Devoted to the Truth: Allāma Amīnī, Author of al-Ghadīr

Dr. Muhammad-Reza Fakhr-Rohani
Foreword by Sheikh Aḥmad Amīnī

Sun Behind the Cloud Publications Ltd

In the Name of Allah, the Beneficent, the Merciful

To Devotees of Truth

Front cover photograph:
Allāma Amīnī at Imam Amīr al-Mu'minīn Public Library, Najaf.

Published by Sun Behind The Cloud Publications
PO Box 15889, Birmingham, B16 6NZ

A CIP catalogue record of this book is available
from the British Library

ISBN (Print): 978-1-908110-58-9
ISBN (eBook): 978-1-908110-59-6

www.sunbehindthecloud.com
info@sunbehindthecloud.com

Contents

A Note on Proper Names and Dates 4

Transliteration Table 5

Preface 7

Acknowledgements 11

Foreword by Sheikh Aḥmad Amīnī 13

PART ONE - The Beginning of Scholarship 17

PART TWO - Authoring *al-Ghadīr* 53

PART THREE - The Quest for Knowledge 98

PART FOUR - A Lasting Legacy 114

Bibliography 144

A Note on Proper Names and Dates

Throughout the present book, place-names often appear without transliterational diacritics and are spelt according to common and contemporary dictionary spellings.

Non-Arab (especially Iranian) family names appear without the preceding Arabic definite article al-. This is retained, however, wherever an Arab figure's name is written.

Allāma 'Abd al-Ḥusayn Amīnī is referred to as 'Abd al-Ḥusayn when speaking of his younger years and then referred to as Allāma Amīnī when speaking of his later life as a scholar.

We have endeavoured to note the death dates of prominent figures throughout the book.

Transliteration Table

ء	ʾ	ز	z	ق	q	Long vowels	
ب	b	س	s	ك	k	ا	ā
ت	t	ش	sh	ل	l	و	ū
ث	th	ص	ṣ	م	m	ي	ī
ج	j	ض	ḍ	ن	n	Short vowels	
ح	ḥ	ط	ṭ	ه	h	ـَ	a
خ	kh	ظ	ẓ	و	w	ـُ	u
د	d	ع	ʿ	ي	y	ـِ	i
ذ	dh	غ	gh	ة	ah		
ر	r	ف	f	ال	al		

Preface

The eleven-volume Tehran edition of the late Allāma Amīnī's *al-Ghadīr* has always had a special place in my father's private library at home. My father is a cleric and we live in Qom, but as a child, I didn't quite understand the discussions of the grown ups, and I was particularly perplexed as to why my father and his clerical friends and colleagues would talk so highly of *al-Ghadīr*. My confusion didn't last long; as I grew up and began learning some Arabic, I realized that the object of their fascination was not simply a book, but rather a highly specialized encyclopedia, of which only eleven volumes have been published. The more I turned its pages, the more marvels I discovered within it. What made *al-Ghadīr* special was more than mere scholarship; I could see that the work was a token of the author's ardent devotion to Imam 'Alī's Divinely-determined right to leadership, which has been inseparably linked with the historic event at Ghadīr Khumm.

By devoting his intellectual energy and enthusiasm to illuminating the right of Imam 'Alī, the late Allāma Amīnī undoubtedly received his reward from the unique personality about whom he developed his book. Today, it is unlikely that any conscientious researcher of Islamic doctrine and history, or any scholar who looks into the character of Imam 'Alī could overlook Allāma Amīnī's *al-Ghadīr*. In this way, a triad has been formed in which Imam 'Alī, Ghadīr Khumm, and Allāma Amīnī are fundamentally bonded.

It was some time after I had first become familiar with *al-Ghadīr* that the ex-Baathist rule under Saddam Hussein collapsed, meaning that I finally had the opportunity to take my first pilgrimage to the sacred shrines of Iraq. It was in the winter of 2006 and the first night of our arrival coincided with the eve of Ashura. For much of our trip, we stayed in Karbala, where we were blessed with the honour of staying in the precincts of Imam al-Ḥusayn's sacred shrine. It was soon after we reached Najaf to visit the shrine of Imam 'Alī that I enquired about the location of the famous library which Allāma Amīnī had established in the city. The Imam Amīr al-Mu'minīn Public Library was close enough to the shrine, that I found it within a few minutes. Now, after several years, I realise that my first visit to the library had such a long-lasting impression on my mind that I cannot regard it as an ordinary trip; it was indeed a research pilgrimage in its own right. In retrospect, I feel that visit brought with it a revolutionary change to the course of my academic life.

To this day, I vividly remember the welcoming atmosphere within the library. As soon as I entered, I encountered the familiar, heart-warming scent of scholarship, and I could feel the power of its founder's ardent devotion to the house of Prophet Muḥammad ever-present in the aroma. Among the shelves crammed full of books, the oldest ones were bound in traditional Iranian and Iraqi leather bindings. These were the very same works that the late Allāma Amīnī used to develop his own books; which he had acquired through his various trips to other and certainly much larger research libraries all around the world. During the days I was in Najaf, I used to visit the Library and became enchanted by its print holdings in various languages, from Arabic to Persian and English. The impact of scholarship displayed in this library seemed unique to any other I had experienced.

Leaving Najaf at the end of my first trip proved a really painful experience. I knew I would miss Imam 'Alī's sacred shrine and the first library in Najaf to be named after him.

Soon after returning home to Qum, I contacted a close friend who knew the youngest son of the late Allāma, Dr. Muḥammad Amīnī, and I was able speak with him in Tehran. A few moments after hanging up the telephone, I received a call from another of Allāma's sons, Sheikh Aḥmad Amīnī, who had long been a resident in Qum. I met with Sheikh Aḥmad at his house a few days later and our first meeting quickly developed into close friendship. Little by little, I came to know more about the character and career of the late Allāma Amīnī, a man who devoted his life to the cause of promoting the ideals of the house of Prophet Muḥammad.

For the most outstanding scholars, it is not only their books but also their lives which guide people. It therefore seems appropriate to attempt to tell the life story of Allāma 'Abd al-Ḥusayn Amīnī, who was indeed an accomplished scholar and a true devotee to the house of Prophet Muḥammad and an ardent scholar who devoted his life to the life of the first Infallible, Imam 'Alī.

It is believed that the present biography of Allāma Amīnī is the first book-length sketch of his life in English[1]. In producing this, my hope is that a wide international readership will be able to benefit from becoming familiar with the life of the Allāma.

---

1. Several books have been published in Arabic and Persian about the life of Allama Amīnī, although not all are equally reliable. Of note is the biography written by Allama Amīnī's son, Ayatollah Sheikh Riḍā Amīnī. Written in Arabic, the focus of Sheikh Riḍā's biography is on the scholarly contribution of his father. Another account written by Sheikh Riḍā, broader in focus, has been written but so far remains unpublished. A shorter biography, also in Arabic, by Ayatollah Sayyid Muḥammad-Ṣādiq Baḥr al-'Ulūm (d. 1399 AH/ 1978) is also of note. On the life of Allama Amīnī in English, only a short encyclopedic entry exists, see Hamid Algar, "Amīnī, Shaikh 'Abd al-Hosayn" *Encyclopaedia Iranica*, vol. 1 (New York, 1985), pp. 955-56.

Other than presenting a sketch of the life and times of the late Allāma, this book also seeks to present pages of early Islamic history as unfolded by the late Allāma in his magnum opus, *al-Ghadīr*. Over time, various events of early Islamic history have been distorted and covered up by the insincere and sinister hands; Allāma Amīnī sought to manifest the truth by differentiating it from the falsehood out of devotion. My wish, then, is for readers to not only learn from the religious and scholarly life of Allāma Amīnī, but also to be inspired by his character and benefit from his truth-seeking scholarship and research methodology.

May the present work be reckoned as a token of my veneration for Prophet Muḥammad and his infallible household and descendants, particularly the immediate successor to Prophet Muḥammad and the Infallible Imam 'Alī. Amen!

Acknowledgements

I would like to express my appreciation to the descendants of the late Allāma 'Abd al-Ḥusayn Amīnī-Najafī for their sincere and unfailing cooperation while this biography was being written. I cannot forget the crucial help I received from my close friend, Sheikh Aḥmad Amīnī-Najafī, the eldest remaining son of the late Allāma Amīnī, who wrote the foreword for this book and provided insightful anecdotes and invaluable observations of his father's character. Next, I would like to thank Mr. Ḥusayn Amīnī-Najafī, Mr. Ja'far Amīnī, and Sheikh Muḥsin Ākhūndī whose answers to some of my queries proved invaluable. Although I never contacted his brother Dr. 'Abbās Ākhūndī, I appreciate his answers that I received via his brother Sheikh Muḥsin Ākhūndī. My appreciation also goes to Mr. 'Alī and Mr. 'Abd al-Ḥusayn Amīnī-Najafī (both of them are sons of the late Ayatollah Dr. Muḥammad-Hadī Amīnī-Najafī).

Further to those already mentioned above, I am grateful to the following for their help while the present work was in gestation: Mr. Muḥammad-Riḍā Ḥakīmī, Mr. Muḥammad Mujtahidī, Dr. Mahdī Mujtahidī, Dr. Ḥaydar Maḥallātī, Ayatollah Sayyid Hādī Rafī'īpūr, Mr. 'Alī Nikzād, Sayyid 'Alī Ṭabāṭabā'ī Yazdī, Sayyid Muḥammad Ṭabāṭabā'ī Yazdī, Dr. 'Abd al-Ḥusayn Ṭāli'ī, Murtaḍā Ḥā'irīzādih, Ayatollah Riḍā Mukhtārī, Aṣghar Muṣṭafawī, Ibrāhīm Shād-Mubārakī, Firishtih Qanbarī, Muḥammad-Ḥusayn Afrākhtih, Ayatollah Murtaḍā Farajpūr, Sheikh Ḥāmid Farajpūr, the late Ayatollah Muḥammad-Ṣādiq Najmī, Samānih Bīglar, Muṣṭafā Niẓāmābādī, Muḥammad Raḥīmī, Muḥammad-'Alī Fallāḥ, Afsānih Namāzī, Muḥsin Amīnī, Hānī Kabīr, Jawād Ṣabāḥī, 'Alī-Akbar Aḥmadlū, Sayyid Muḥammad Mīr-Nāṣirī,

Mīnā Uskūyī, Amīr-Jābir Ṭāhirī, Ibrāhīm Zāri'ī, Manṣūrih Fāḍilī, 'Alī-Riḍā Ilhāmī, Akbar Chirāghī, Dr. Fāṭimih Towfīqī, Dr. Riḍā Karīmī, Dr. Muḥammad-Ḥusayn A'rābī, Ms. Liylā 'Azīzpūr-Shīrfurūsh, Dr. Ḥasan Miqyāsī, Dr. Sayyid Riḍā Mu'addab, Ayatollah Sayyid Hādī Khusrowshāhī (Iran), Majīd Banā'ī, Parīsā Gulistānī, Sheikh 'Abd al-Ḥamīd Muṭahharī (Afghanistan), the late Prof. Dr. Sayyid Hosain Mohammad Jafri, Dr. Muḥammad-Reza Kazimi, Sayyid 'Alī-Riḍā Kāẓimī (Pakistan), Dr. Mohammad Abbas Rizvi, Sayyid Aejaz 'Alī Torab Ḥusayn al-Ḥusaynī Bhujwala, the late Prof. Dr. Sayyid Sadiq Naqvi (India), the late Ayatollah Sheikh Bāqir Sharīf al-Qarashī, Rā'id al-Baṣrī, Ayatollah Sayyid Muḥammad Mahdī al-Mūsawī al-Khirsān, Dr. Yaḥyā Nūrī Khalaf, Hudā al-Karbalā'ī, Dr. Sayyid Salmān Hādī Āl Ṭu'mah (Iraq), Prof. Dr. Sebastian Guenther, Dr. Mareike Beez (Germany), Dr. Zuzka Černa (Czech Republic), Dr. Tressy Arts, Mrs. Tehseen Fatema Merali (UK), Dr. Yitzhak Nakash, Dr. Michael Cook, Dr. Marcia K. Hermansen, Dr. John Andrew Morrow (USA); Dr. Anṭun Bārā (Syria/Kuwait), Prof. Hans Renders (The Netherlands), Dr. Hamid Mavani, Prof. Dr. Liaqat Ali Takim (Canada); Yūsuf Kattani, the Rev. Dr. Peter Ford (Lebanon/USA); and Dr. Jason Thompson (Egypt/USA).

Last but not least, I owe a great and special debt of gratitude to my family, particularly to my wife, without whose profound understanding and exemplary cooperation the completion of this biography could not have been accomplished. I pray to Allah to record the religious rewards of developing such a book in her profile of deeds. Amen!

Dr. Muhammad-Reza Fakhr-Rohani
June 2019
Qum

Foreword

by Sheikh Ahmad Amīnī

It is my great pleasure to see the first book-length English biography of my late father, Allāma ʻAbd al-Ḥusayn Amīnī. Looking back on the life of my father, I see two striking characteristics: his love of the Creator and creation, and his love of scholarship.

Allāma Amīnī was a real altruist; he loved everybody purely for the sake of loving Allah. As a sincere devotee of Allah, he was at the service of people. He believed that it was his Islamic education, particularly those pearls of wisdom of the sixth Infallible, Imam Jaʻfar al-Ṣādiq, which inspired him in his service. Rather than boast about being a high-ranking religious figure, he regarded himself as a normal individual like any other. He maintained that a love of Allah accompanied by a staunch belief in the superiority of the devotees of Allah, have a profound impact on the human character.

Allāma Amīnī would work more than seventeen hours a day. If it were other than this, he would not have been so successful in his scholarly and social endeavours, as those involved in research will testify. His establishment of the Imam Amīr al-Mu'minīn Public Library of Najaf was rooted in his love for people. He symbolized the best manifestations of love for Prophet Muḥammad and his household.

Allāma Amīnī believed that there had been a trend of misleading masses in the history of Muslims. Leading

Meccan polytheists who barely believed in Islam pretended to accept it as their new faith. Yet, they devised several ways to counteract against the true version of Islam. They decided to de-sanctify, hence socio-religiously, defame and de-authorize whosoever proved to be the true believer in the Prophet Moḥammad, even his closest relatives and his staunch companions. On the other hand, certain people who were enemies started to be portrayed as holders of important offices in the Islamic era, such as a special scribe of the Prophet. To initiate this carefully devised plot, certain (pseudo)experts of religious education were trained to pave the way for this perilous policy. To regain and safeguard their former, pre-Islamic socio-economic power, it proved essential for them to superficially theorize the basis of their economic power and social status. To make the most of the Islamic religion for their interests and benefits, they have fabricated their own divisions, or disciplines, of Islamic religious studies, namely, theology, Qur'an interpretation, and history, all within the realm of their political courts and power.

However appealing and sacred they might appear, such disciplines would certainly deceive the masses. In this way, jurisprudence and its basic tenets had been reshaped (in contrast to the teachings of the Infallibles), hence they prove chiefly, if not entirely, stiff and largely devoid of the didactic (moral-cum-educational) aspects.

In the history of Muslim peoples and lands, such prejudiced rulers and major policy-makers prevented the truth-seeking and optimistic masses from having direct and easy access to the teachings of the Infallibles. Rather, they falsified the truths so drastically that masses came to regard the Infallibles as no longer reliable, hence started opposing them and taking revenge from them for obscuring the real face of Islam. These covert policies and instigations were carefully devised and realised.

Allāma Amīnī regarded it as his mission to prove this major deviation that has taken place in the history of Islam shortly after the demise of the Prophet Moḥammad. Allāma Amīnī never intended to add fuel to the fire of the centuries-long schism between Sunnis and Shiites. Through such clarifications, he invited not only all Muslims but all intellectuals of any faith to discern the truth and to understand the real scenario.

My father was a symbol of devotion to the Islamic religion, people, and scholarship. Certainly, the life of such a personality demands consideration into his upbringing, education, inspiration, and activities in the service of others.

I am most grateful to Allah that I have become acquainted with my father's biographer, Dr. Muhammad-Reza Fakhr-Rohani, an erudite scholar in his own right with several of his own works. I sincerely appreciate his efforts on behalf of both myself and all of the descendants of Allāma Amīnī. I am also grateful to Sun Behind the Cloud Publications for undertaking the publication of this biography.

PART ONE

THE BEGINNING OF SCHOLARSHIP

"He who gives a great deal of thought to what he learns masters his knowledge, and comes to understand that which he could not understand before"

-IMAM ʿALĪ

Family Tree

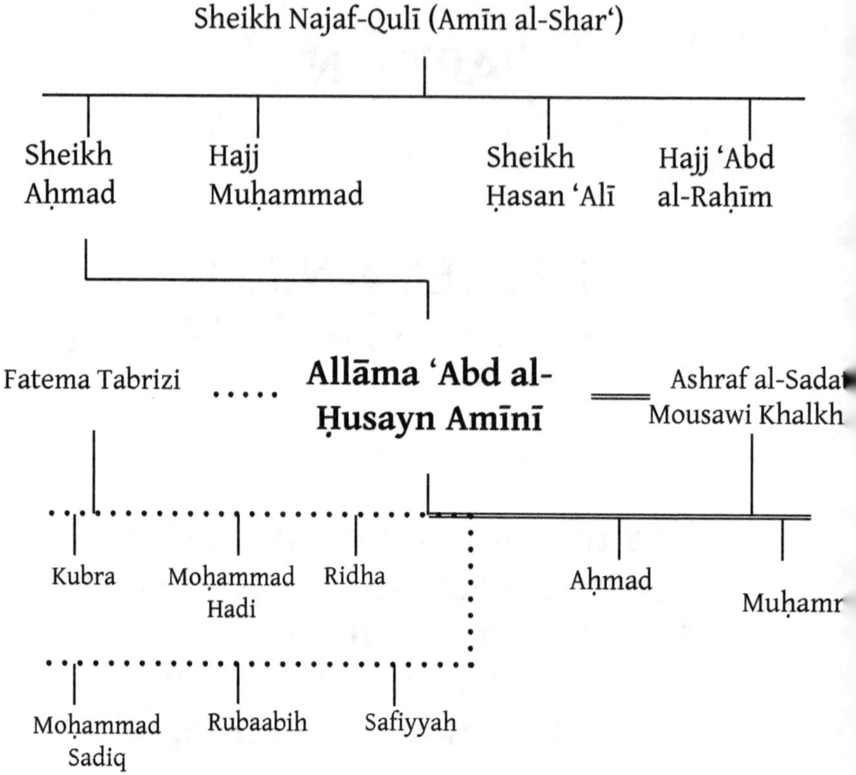

····· Denotes first marriage

═══ Denotes second marriage

His Forefathers

Much is known about Allāma Amīnī's family going back to his paternal grandfather, Sheikh Najaf-Qulī, but beyond that there is less information. Najaf-Qulī was born in 1257 AH/ 1841 in Sardahā, a village located to the south of Sarāb, which was a small town. In 1304 AH/ 1886, Najaf-Qulī migrated from his village eastward to Tabriz, in northwestern Iran. He was the son of Sheikh 'Abd Allāh, a man known for the letters he wrote using the pen name (*takhalluṣ*) 'Sarmast', meaning 'one profoundly enchanted'. Sheikh 'Abd Allāh was the son of Hajj Muḥammad, son of Allāh-Yār, son of Muḥammad.

Najaf-Qulī was commonly known by the honorific title 'Amīn al-Shar'', meaning 'trustee of the (Islamic) path and law'. He was keen to seek knowledge and would often associate with the learned people of Tabriz. A religiously devout figure, Najaf-Qulī was also a skilful calligrapher, as well as a competent poet. Some specimens of his calligraphy feature his prayers and supplications. His own pen name was '*Wāthiq*', an Arabic word which means 'the one who is dependent on Allah'. The gemstone of his ring bore the inscription *al-wāthiq bi Allāh al-Ghanīyy, 'abduhū Najaf-Qulī*, that is, 'the Dependant of Allah the Sufficient, his servant Najaf-Qulī'.

Sheikh Najaf-Qulī used to study in Najaf for some time and kept good relations with the leading Shia authorities of Najaf, who knew him well. When he passed away in 1340 AH / 1921, his body was taken from Tabriz to Najaf so that he could be buried in the Wādī al-Salām Cemetery, a vast graveyard not far from Imam 'Alī's shrine.

Najaf-Qulī had four sons, Sheikh Aḥmad, Hajj Muḥammad,[1] Sheikh Ḥasan 'Alī 'Fakhr',[2] and Hajj 'Abd al-Raḥīm.[3] Of these sons, it was Sheikh Aḥmad who later became the father of Allāma Amīnī.

Sheikh Aḥmad was born in Sardahā (1287 AH/ 1870), and was tutored by his father in Persian and Arabic. When the family moved to Tabriz, he continued his education under the great scholars of Tabriz such as Mirza Asad Allāh b. Muḥsin Tabrīzī.[4] Sheikh Aḥmad obtained Licenses for Transmission (*ijāzas*) from some leading *mujtahids* such as Sheikh 'Alī Shīrāzī Gharawī[5] and Sheikh 'Alī Īrawānī Gharawī[6]. It was these last two scholars who, alongside Tabriz's great mujtahid Ayatollah Sayyid Abū al-Ḥasan Angajī Tabrīzī[7], endorsed Sheikh Aḥmad's status as a *mujtahid* in his own right. This meant that Sheikh Aḥmad was qualified to derive religious laws, through his own independent reasoning, from the fundamental sources of Islam and, above all, from the Holy Qur'an. Having studied under a number of leading *mujtahids* in Tabriz and having already made a name for himself as a Shia cleric, Sheikh Aḥmad went on to earn *ijāzas* from several leading scholars in Najaf.[8]

1. d. 1377 AH/ 1957
2. date of death unknown
3. d. 1375 AH/ 1955
4. d. 1325 AH/ 1906
5. d. 1355 AH/ 1936
6. d. 1354 AH/ 1935
7. d. 1357 AH / 1938
8. Some of those who provided him with Licenses for Transmission (*ijāzas*) include Ayatollah Asad Allāh b. Muḥsin Bazzāz Tabrīzī (d. 1325 AH/ 1907), Ayatollah Sayyid Mirza 'Alī Shīrāzī (d. 1355 AH/ 1936), Ayatollah Sayyid Abū al-Ḥasan Mūsawī Iṣfahānī (d. 1365 AH/ 1945), Ayatollah Muḥammad-Ḥusayn Gharawī Iṣfahānī (d. 1361 AH/ 1942), Ayatollah 'Alī Īrawānī (d. 1354 AH/ 1935), Ayatollah Mirza Raḍī b.

Sheikh Aḥmad was a close friend of the late Ayatollah Sheikh 'Alī Khīyābānī[1] the author of *Waqāyi' al-ayyām*. He also maintained fruitful relationships with Ayatollah Gharawī Iṣfahānī, and other scholarly figures of Najaf and Karbala.

The Licenses for Transmission (*ijāzas*) Sheikh Aḥmad received throughout his life fell broadly into two groups. In the first, there were several licences relating to the socio-economic issues of the time, such as the ways in which charitable donations were distributed for the benefit of the poor. The second group of licences entitled him to relate, explain, translate, and teach lessons on Shia hadiths narrated from the Prophet and select members of his descendants. He was granted permission to relate hadiths from many important scholars[2].

Muḥammad-Ḥasan Zunūzī Tabrīzī (d. 1360 AH/ 1941), Ayatollah Aḥmad Qarachahdaghī Tabrīzī (date of death unknown), Ayatollah Fattāḥ Shahīdī (d. 1372 AH/ 1952), and Ayatollah Mirza Khalīl-Āqā (d. 1368 AH/ 1948).

1. d. 1367 AH/ 1947

2. These scholars included: Ayatollah Sayyid Mirza 'Alī Shīrāzī (d. 1936), Ayatollah Sayyid Abū al-Ḥasan Mūsawī Iṣfahānī (d. 1945), Ayatollah Sheikh Muḥammad-Ḥusayn Gharawī Iṣfahānī (d. 1942), Ayatollah Sayyid Ḥusayn Ṭabāṭabā'ī Burūjirdī (d. 1960), Ayatollah Sheikh Mirza 'Alī Īrawānī (d. 1935), Ayatollah Mirza Raḍī Zunūzī Tabrīzī (d. 1941), Ayatollah Mirza Aḥmad Mujtahid Tabrīzī (date of death unknown), Ayatollah Mirza Fattāḥ Shahīdī (d. 1952), and Ayatollah Mirza Khalīl Āqā Mujtahid (d. 1941). The last of these teachers, Ayatollah Shahīdī, was an eminent graduate of the Najaf seminary (ḥawzah) where he studied with Ayatollah Sheikh 'Alī-Akbar Nahāwandī (d. 1949), Ayatollah Muḥammad-Kāẓim Khurāsānī (d. 1911), and Ayatollah Sheikh Abū al-Qāsim Urdūbādī (d. 1914).

When Sheikh Aḥmad was studying, printed books were hardly available in Iran and Iraq. With many important works still in manuscript form, the most common way of acquiring a work was through having them transcribed, either by hiring a copyist, or transcribing the text oneself. While copyists were adept at writing quickly, they did not always manage to avoid errors, whether through lack of care or lack of understanding of the text. As such, Sheikh Aḥmad preferred to copy out the texts he required himself and, throughout his lifetime, he transcribed several books and treatises.

A number of noteworthy works feature amongst the books Sheikh Aḥmad transcribed, including the *Kitāb ṣifāt al-shīʿah* of Abū Jaʿfar Muḥammad b. ʿAlī b. Bābawayh al-Qummī "Sheikh al-Ṣadūq".[1] *Sharḥ qaṣīdah al-ashbāḥ* by Sheikh Abū ʿAbd Allāh al-Mufajjaʿ[2] was a commentary on a 119-couplet poem by the Iraqi poet, Abū ʿAbd Allāh Muḥammad b. Aḥmad b. ʿAbd Allāh al-Baṣrī, in praise of the devotees of the first infallible, Imam ʿAlī. In 1354 AH/ 1935. Sheikh Aḥmad transcribed the ode and presented a copy of it to the great Iraqi author and scholar, Sheikh Muḥammad Ṭāhir al-Samāwī[3]. Sheikh al-Samāwī made a copy of the ode and returned it to Sheikh Aḥmad's son, Allāma Amīnī. Āqā Buzurg tells us of a letter of appreciation found in the papers of Allāma Amīnī which was written in 1354 AH/ 1935 in Najaf by Sheikh al-Samāwī addressed to Sheikh Aḥmad in Tabriz.[4]

---

1. d. 381 AH/ 991
2. d. 327 AH/ 938
3. d. 1370 AH/ 1950
4. See Ayatollah Sheikh Āqā Buzurg Ṭihrānī, *al-Dharīʿah ilā taṣānīf al-Shīʿah*;, Najaf, 1381 AH / 1961; Qum, 1408 AH / 1987 (25 vols.); vol. 14, pp. 4-5, no. 1487.

In 1354 AH/ 1935 Sheikh Aḥmad transcribed *Kitāb al-'arūs* of Abū Muḥammad Ja'far b. 'Alī b. Aḥmad al-Qummī and *Mishkāt al-anwār fī ghurar al-akhbār* by Abū al-Faḍl 'Alī al-Ṭabarasī[1] in 1357 AH / 1938.

As might be expected, the private library of Sheikh Aḥmad was a treasure filled with fine books which celebrated a wide variety of scholarship. It was well known amongst scholars and intellectuals for its priceless holdings. The collection of printed volumes and hand-written manuscripts was eventually donated to the Imam Amīr al-Mu'minīn Public Library of Najaf. They have formed a cornerstone of research for future generations.

In addition to transcribing and collecting written works, Sheikh Aḥmad authored many books on various topics within Shia scholarship, including a commentary on the *Makāsib* of the late Sheikh Murtaḍā Anṣārī[2]. This work was particularly celebrated; the prominent *mujtahid* and exemplary bibliographer, Ayatollah Sheikh Āqā Buzurg Ṭihrānī, lists Sheikh Aḥmad's commentary in his celebrated work of Shia bibliography, *al-Dharī'ah ilā taṣānīf al-shī'ah* (see vol. 1, p. 124), and the prominent Sunni researcher, 'Umar Riḍā Kaḥḥāla, mentions Sheikh Aḥmad's commentary in his *Mu'jam al-mu'allifin*, (see vol. 2, p. 193).

Another of Sheikh Aḥmad's popular works was his commentary on *al-Lum'ah al-Dimashqīyyah* by Zayn al-Dīn al-'Āmilī who was martyred in 965 AH/ 1557, and is better known as Shahīd al-Thānī (the 'Second Martyr'). Preserved in the manuscripts section of the Imām Amīr al-Mu'minīn Public Library, this commentary contains precise elucidatory remarks on the realm of Shia jurisprudence (*fiqh*).

1. d. early 7th/13th cent.
2. d. 1281 AH/ 1864

In addition to authoring these two commentaries, Sheikh Aḥmad also edited two literary anthologies. One anthology is a collection of didactic Persian literature produced by outstanding literary, religious, and social figures. The work is contained in 175 folios, and was completed in 1307 AH/ 1889. The second anthology pertains to both Arabic and Persian literatures. A slim manuscript of 46 folios, the work catalogues short texts, apophthegms, and aphorisms from notable figures. Sheikh Aḥmad finished this work in 1328 AH/ 1910.

In the field of jurisprudence, Sheikh Aḥmad edited a manuscript which records thirty jurisprudential queries directed toward the late Ayatollah Sayyid Muḥammad-Kāẓim Ṭabāṭabā'ī Yazdī[1] along with the Ayatollah's responses. This collection takes the form of 10 folios.

In addition to being a remarkable scholar, Sheikh Aḥmad was a generous, good-tempered, and pious man. It is said that he seldom became irritated unless an open affront was made against Islamic religious standards. He was a prominent figure of Tabriz, leading congregational prayers, reciting marriage vows for young couples, and acting as both a jurist and a judge. He was also financially self-sufficient through the crops he grew on farmlands he owned. Sheikh Aḥmad had four sons, Hajj Maḥmūd[2] , Sheikh 'Abd al-Ḥusayn (the subject of this biography), Mirza Ibrāhīm[3], and Muḥsin, who sadly passed away at a young age. Hajj Maḥmūd was a merchant first in Tabriz and later on in Tehran, and lived a long life. Mirza Ibrāhīm, commonly referred to as Ibrāhīm Aḥmad al-Amīnī al-Najafī, wrote the book *Ā'īnih-yi*

1. d. 1337 AH/ 1918
2. d. 1412 AH/ 1991
3. d. 1403 AH/ 1982

hidāyat wa ithbāt-i wilāyat az naẓar-i Qur'an wa sunnat (3 vols., Tehran, 1392 AH/ 1350 Sh/ 1972). Of his sons, it was 'Abd al-Ḥusayn Amīnī who became a prominent figure in the realm of Islamic scholarship.

Sheikh Aḥmad became ill in the last months of his life. He was brought to Tehran for medical treatment and was hospitalized there. He passed away in Tehran in 1370 AH/ 1950. His body was taken to Qum for burial in the Qabristān-i Now (The New Cemetery) which is close to the shrine of Lady Fāṭimah al-Ma'ṣūmah.

The Early Years

Born in Tabriz in 1320 AH/ 1902 to Sheikh Aḥmad Amīnī and Mrs. Ruqayyih, 'Abd al-Ḥusayn (literally, 'Servant of Ḥusayn') bore a name that demonstrated the religious commitment of his parents and their devotion to the third Infallible Imam al-Ḥusayn who was martyred in Karbala, 61 AH/ 680. 'Abd al-Ḥusayn's mother was careful in the way she raised her children; she would breastfeed them in a state of having performed ritual ablution (*wuḍū*) and cultivate a religious atmosphere in their home. It was here, in Sayyidlar Lane, off Mārālān Street in the Ghīyāth District of Tabriz, that 'Abd al-Ḥusayn received his primary education under the tutelage of his father, Sheikh Aḥmad. He received instruction in both Persian and Arabic and was taught the love of Prophet Muḥammad and his infallible progeny as well as those who sacrificed their lives for their noble ideas and ideals.

The Beginning of Scholarship

'Abd al-Ḥusayn continued his education in Madrasa Ṭālibīyyah, one of the religious colleges of Tabriz, which was situated in a convenient location in the old bazaar, and was established in the second half of the 11th centuary by Mirza Ṭālib Khan, son of Hajj Isḥāq Khan. The Ṭālibīyyah Madrasa (in Persian *Madrasiy-i Ṭālibīyyah*) was well respected, attracting both prominent *mujtahids* aspiring to disseminate the knowledge they had acquired, and many donations from the pious since 1087 AH/ 1676. In 1367 AH/ 1947 some of the dilapidated buildings of the school had to be rebuilt.

'Abd al-Ḥusayn attended the lessons and lectures of several *mujtahids* of Tabriz at the Madrasa Ṭālibīyyah, keen to reach the level of his teachers. One such prominent figure was Ayatollah Sayyid Muḥammad b. 'Abd al-Karīm Mūsawī[1]. Known as '*Mawlānā*', Ayatollah Mūsawī had studied in Najaf from 1312 AH to 1321 AH (1894–1903), and became a high-ranking *mujtahid* who had expertise in Qur'anic exegesis, interpretation as well as jurisprudence and the principles of jurisprudence.

'Abd al-Ḥusayn also studied with Ayatollah Sayyid Murtaḍā b. Aḥmad b. Muḥammad Ḥusaynī Khusrowshāhī[2], a renowned mujtahid of Tabriz, whose book *Ihdā' al-ḥaqīr fī ma'nā ḥadīth al-ghadīr ilā akhīh al-bāri' al-baṣīr* was well known.[3] The work must have impressed 'Abd al-Ḥusayn

1. d. 1363 AH/ 1943

2. d. 1372 AH/ 1953

3. *Ihdā' al-ḥaqīr fī ma'nā ḥadīth al-ghadīr ilā akhīh al-bāri' al-baṣīr*, ed. Sayyid Hādī Khusrowshāhī; Najaf, 1353 AH / 1934. More recent editions, ed. Sayyid Murtaḍā Ḥusaynī Khusrowshāhī, have been published

since it dealt with the concept of *walīy* and *mawlā* in the context of the Prophet's declaration at Ghadīr Khumm, a captivating event that took place in the early Islamic period which 'Abd al-Ḥusayn would devote much of his life to discussing.[1]

'Abd al-Ḥusayn had other prominent teachers in Tabriz. Among them, there were Ayatollah Sheikh Ḥusayn b. 'Abd 'Alī Tūtūnchī[2] and Ayatollah 'Alī Aṣghar Malikī.[3] Both of them were *mujtahids*; the former earned his permission to practice *ijtihad* in Najaf where he resided for eleven years and the latter migrated to Najaf later in life where he remained until his death and was buried there.

'Abd al-Ḥusayn was a devoted student, seizing every single moment to add to his knowledge. He knew, however, that it was Najaf, not Tabriz, that was the renowned centre for Islamic religious scholarship in the Shia world. Even though at that time, taking long-distance journeys was especially difficult and dangerous, 'Abd al-Ḥusayn felt that benefiting from the scholarly atmosphere of Najaf and relocating himself, away from Tabriz was a risk worth taking. Having barely reached puberty, 'Abd al-Ḥusayn decided to leave for Najaf, without informing his parents, by joining a

---

in Qum in 1398 AH / 1356 Sh / 1977 and 1386 Sh/ 2007.

1. I owe this insight to Ayatollah Sayyid Hādī Khusrowshāhī, son of the late Ayatollah Sayyid Murtaḍā Khusrowshāhī, who explained it to me in a telephone interview on 21 April 2015. The same point is indicated in his preliminary remark on the new edition of the *Festschrift* published in honour of the late Allama Amīnī. See, Sayyid Hādī Khusrowshāhī, 'Ishārih', in *Yād nāmih-yi Allama Amīnī*, ed. by Sayyid Ja'far Shahīdī and Muḥammad-Riḍā Ḥakīmī; Qum, new edn., Qum, 1390 Sh/ 2011, p. 14.

2. d. 1360 AH/ 1941

3. d. unknown

caravan of pilgrims who intended to visit the sacred shrine cities of Iraq, including Najaf. Naturally, his absence for three days was a cause of serious distress for his parents. By quizzing 'Abd al-Ḥusayn's classmates and close friends, Sheikh Aḥmad managed to find his son after a few days and brought him back to Tabriz.

Sheikh Aḥmad took this event seriously and promised to help his son and enable him reach Najaf to study and research in time. The young 'Abd al-Ḥusayn was so intensely devoted that he would burst into tears whenever he thought about Najaf and the shrine of Imam 'Alī. Not long after this, it became clear that 'Abd al-Ḥusayn could no longer remain in Tabriz - his heart was in Najaf. He was already a true lover of both knowledge and spirituality, and Najaf offered him the opportunity to be immersed in both.

Allāma Amīnī's Love for his Parents and Devotion to Seeking Knowledge

Allāma Amīnī's brother, Hajj Ibrāhīm, was both a businessman and a scholar. He wrote a book as an expression of his love for Imam 'Alī entitled *The Mirror in Spotting Wilayah* (in English paraphrase). He narrates that one day the three brothers were sitting with their father and reading introductory books on Islam. Their father asked a question to which none of the brothers had a response, so their father, whilst asking why they could not answer, became angry with them. 'Abd al-Ḥusayn (Allāma Amīnī) became upset and left to go to a quiet place, so Hajj Ibrāhīm followed him thinking that they could joke together and cheer each other up. He found that Allāma, was still very upset, and had retreated to the cellar.

When Hajj Ibrahim went to visit Allāma years later in Najaf, he saw his brother in a whole new light. Allāma was speaking to scholars confidently, debating with them, holding discussions, all the while quoting traditions which he backed up with sources and page numbers. He was very surprised, as he knew that his brother did not have a strong memory.

When he asked his brother what he had done to transform his memory, Allāma replied by asking if he remembered the time when their father had asked them a question that none of them knew the answer to. After Hajj Ibrāhīm replied that he did remember, Allāma continued to explain that on that day he had asked Allah to grant him a good memory so that he could make their parents happy and to make use of his expert knowledge for disseminating Islamic knowledge.

Hajj Ibrāhīm commented that after that day, until the end of their lives, his parents were always most comfortable at Allāma's house and during their old age and illnesses, they would retreat to Allāma's house. This was the extent to which Allāma's deal with Allah had come into effect.

Between Najaf and Tabriz

At the beginning of the twentieth century, as a result of the Iranian Constitutional Revolution and the First World War, Tabriz became the centre of political upheavals and economic hardship. The prevailing ideas were not always in harmony with Shia teaching. Despite this precarious environment, 'Abd al-Ḥusayn completed his elementary level seminary studies. This is a testament to the stable and sound Islamic religious atmosphere his parents provided him at home.

Having completed his elementary studies, 'Abd al-Ḥusayn left for Najaf in 1336 AH/ 1917, at the age of fourteen, to pursue his dream of studying in Najaf. He was accompanied by his paternal grandfather, Najaf-Qulī, and was taken to see the leading religious authorities of Najaf, who promised to look after him. Najaf-Qulī was a *mujtahid* who had studied extensively in Najaf, and had become familiar with the religious authorities there.

Najaf was more desirable than Tabriz by far, not just academically, but also religiously. For the devotee, the appeal of Najaf included its own shrine, as well as the access it gave to the other shrine cities of Iraq, including Karbala. Here, 'Abd al-Ḥusayn paid homage to Imam al-Ḥusayn and, al-'Abbās b. 'Alī, along with all the other martyrs of 10 Muharram 61 AH/681, before returning to Najaf to commence his advanced (*khārij*) studies.

For an individual who was raised in the climate of the southern Caucasus, the scorching summer heat of Najaf proved unbearable. To escape it, 'Abd al-Ḥusayn would return to Tabriz for the summer months. This lifestyle between Najaf and Tabriz continued for eight years, during which 'Abd al-Ḥusayn became a close disciple to a number of renowned *mujtahids*, who proved to significantly influence his thoughts. These were scholars such as Ayatollah Sayyid Muḥammad b. Muḥammad Bāqir Ḥusaynī Fīrūzābādī,[1] famous for his exemplary piety; Ayatollah Sayyid Abū Turāb b. Abū al-Qāsim Khūnsārī[2] who was a distinguished and talented scholar with expertise in jurisprudence, hadith scholarship, arithmetic, mathematics, geometry, and geography; Ayatollah 'Alī Īrawānī[3] and Ayatollah Abū al-Ḥasan Mishkīnī[4] a leading figure in issues of Islamic doctrine and creed.

After qualifying as a *mujtahid* in around 1344 AH/1925, 'Abd al-Ḥusayn received a letter from his father and relocated to Tabriz as Sheikh 'Abd al-Ḥusayn. This tall, handsome, and youthful figure was welcomed by his relatives, old classmates, friends, and neighbours, as it would have been customary for anybody who has returned from a pilgrimage. But Sheikh 'Abd al-Ḥusayn was now a scholar as well as a pilgrim, a figure who attracted a large number of guests.

One notable guest during the first days of Sheikh 'Abd al-Ḥusayn's homecoming was a previous teacher of his: Ayatollah Hajj Maḥmūd Dūzdūzānī.[5] Pleased to find his former student a cleric and already an outstanding researcher, Ayatollah Dūzdūzānī suggested that Sheikh 'Abd al-Ḥusayn

1. d. 1345/1926

2. d. 1346 AH/1927
3. d. 1354 AH/1935
4. d. 1358 AH/1939
5. d. 1369 AH/1949

wear the clerical robe from that day forward. Before he could respond, 'Abd al-Ḥusayn found himself caught in a strange yet wonderful situation. Ayatollah Dūzdūzānī had already ordered a splendid white turban and a cloak for Sheikh 'Abd al-Ḥusayn, and with that, his position as a locally recognized cleric was cemented.

Sheikh 'Abd al-Ḥusayn began to teach in both formal settings to religious students and more informal settings to the public. In the religious schools of Tabriz, especially the Ṭālibīyyah Madrasa, he would teach lessons in Arabic grammar, lexicology, and letters as well as Islamic doctrine. It would have been, no doubt, an honour for his former teachers and his family to see him as a qualified scholar active in the community.

The mosques of Tabriz would send in requests to Sheikh 'Abd al-Ḥusayn to lead congregational prayers and preach. In light of his duty to offer religious guidance in those turbulent days, Allāma resolved to focus on the exegesis of the opening chapter of the Qur'an, the 'Fātiḥa'. The wisdom of his decision is clear: the Fātiḥa is recited in every prayer and every Muslim is expected to know at least an outline of the meaning of what they are reciting. Not only could he give a glimpse into the various levels of literal, metaphorical, and mystical meanings as well as their connotations in the Qur'an, but he could enrich people's experience of a basic Islamic ritual.

Although protective of his time, Sheikh 'Abd al-Ḥusayn was keen to attend the celebratory and commemorative gatherings of the Shia calendar. Whereas in Tabriz he was a preacher, his attendance in Najaf would usually be as a member of the audience. Sheikh 'Abd al-Ḥusayn was a passionate believer in the rights of the Prophet's Infallible household (the Ahl al-Bayt) and would shed tears upon hearing of their afflictions, particularly those which befell Imam 'Alī, Lady Fāṭimah al-Zahrā', and Imam al-Ḥusayn. As is highly recommended in Shia hadiths, Allāma would walk to Karbala on foot to pay homage to Imam al-Ḥusayn and al-'Abbās b. 'Alī.

To elucidate the Qur'anic Sura al-Fātiḥa, Allāma Amīnī drew on the wisdom within hadith literature, and discussed the linguistic and rhetorical aspects of the verses. His lessons formed the basis of *Tafsīr fātiḥat al-kitāb*, published after his death. Although still young, he was also able to author a work of matyrology, *Shuhadā' al-faḍīlah*, which granted him recognition as an "Allāma" (one who is accomplished in fields of Islamic learning beyond jurisprudence) among the scholars of Najaf. During a trip to Tabriz, Ayatollah Muḥammad 'Alī Urdūbādī was able to study *Shuhadā' al-faḍīlah* and was so impressed that he composed an Arabic ode in praise of the book.

Allāma Amīnī had barely stayed in Tabriz for less than two years when the call to Najaf once more became irresistible to him. The spiritual atmosphere of Najaf and the opportunity to advance his studies further overtook the allure of the comfort of familiar surroundings and the respect he received from the people of his city.

Allāma Amīnī married Miss Fāṭimah Tabrīzī in 1301 Sh/1922 in Tabriz, during a summer break from his studies in Najaf. At the time, Allāma Amīnī was 20 years old. His wife was a daughter of the late Hajj Mirza Bāqir Tabrīzī.[1]

They had six children together: three daughters and three sons. The first child was a daughter who was born in 1303

1. d. unknown

Sh/ 1924 and who passed away at the age of 53. Her birth was followed by three sons, Muḥammad-Hādī,[1] Riḍā,[2] and Muḥammad-Ṣādiq.[3] Muḥammad-Ṣādiq lived in Mashhad, while his elder brothers lived in Tehran. The youngest of his children are his two daughters who are still alive today and reside in Qum.

Returning to Najaf at around the age of 23 ahead of his wife, Allāma Amīnī showed great determination to progress, immersing himself in the classes and debates he had missed while in Tabriz. Although never depriving any enquirer of his expertise, he refrained from taking on a great number of students, preferring instead to remain focused on his own learning.

In 1335 Sh/ 1956, Allāma Amīnī also married Miss Ashraf al-Sādāt, a daughter of the late Ayatollah Sayyid 'Alī Mūsawī Khalkhālī who was a renowned Najaf-based Iranian *mujtahid* and scholar. He settled her in Tehran and commuted between Najaf and Tehran a few times a year, mainly during the spring and summer. From his second marriage, Allāma Amīnī had two sons, Aḥmad (b. 1336 Sh/ 1957) and Muḥammad (b. 1342 Sh/ 1963), both born and raised mainly in Tehran.

After several years, Allāma Amīnī became a high-ranking *mujtahid*. His world view was broadened through achieving Licenses for Transmission (*ijāzas*) in various fields of Islamic learning – hadith, history, jurisprudence, and principles of jurisprudence –given to him by his teachers in light of his attainment.

1. d. 1376 Sh/ 1997

2. d. 1391 Sh/ 2012

3. d. 1373 Sh/ 1994

Advice to his son on becoming a scholar

Dr. Muḥammad-Hādī Amīnī, a son of Allāma Amīnī, wrote a book on a theme in Islamic history and presented it to his father to obtain his comments before publishing. After reading the book, Allāma Amīnī provided his comments and guidance. Muḥammad-Hādī expressed his profound love for Allāma, not because of his paternal relation, but due to his scholarly character.

In response, Allāma Amīnī thanked him and advised him to be careful; to not waste his time by attending gatherings held here and there, to devote all his energy and capacity sincerely to the cause of the Holy Qur'an and the Ahl al-Bayt, and to not expect any reward for his scholarly efforts, but instead to make himself ready for maltreatment.

Scholarly Influences

The scholars who influenced Allāma Amīnī during his second stay in Najaf were many. We can list them in approximate order of age as follows.

1. **Ayatollah Sayyid 'Alī Shīrāzī**[1] an expert in Islamic history, Persian and Arabic literature, and Islamic (chiefly Avicennan medicine), as well as Islamic doctrine, Islamic philosophy, jurisprudence, and the principles of jurisprudence. He was son of the late Grand Ayatollah Sayyid Muḥammad-Ḥasan Shīrāzī[2], famous for the fatwa he gave in 1308/1891 against the tobacco concession of Nāṣir al-Dīn Shah to the British which had resulted in forcing the British to withdraw from the tobacco crops of Iran.

2. **Ayatollah Muḥammad-Ḥusayn Nāyinī Najafī**[3] an outstanding figure who shone in the fields of principles of jurisprudence, Shia political thought, and jurisprudence. He studied in the seminary of Isfahan with some of its leading figures. Upon migrating to Iraq, he attended the seminaries of Karbala, Samarra, and Najaf.

3. **Ayatollah 'Abd al-Karīm Ḥā'irī Yazdī**[4] a high-ranking mujtahid and eminent graduate of the seminaries of Samarra, Karbala, and Najaf. He is credited with reviving the centuries-old seminary of Qum.

1. d. 1355 AH/ 1936
2. d. 1312 AH/ 1894
3. d. 1355 AH/ 1936
4. d. 1355 AH/ 1936

4. **Ayatollah Sayyid Abū al-Ḥasan Mūsawī Iṣfahānī**[1] a leading religious authority who received millions of Shia followers and adherents worldwide from Iraq to Iran, Lebanon, Afghanistan, Pakistan and India.

5. **Ayatollah Muḥammad-Ḥusayn Gharawī Iṣfahānī**[2] an accomplished scholar who was not only an unrivalled expert in jurisprudence and the principles of jurisprudence, but was also a wise sage, philosopher, and poet. His expertise was manifest in his Arabic and Persian poems, and he played a key role in the cultural and intellectual development of learned Shia circles in Iraq.

6. **Ayatollah Muḥammad-Ḥusayn Kāshif al-Ghiṭā'**[3] a well-known Arab mujtahid, who was a true intellectual, a profound philosopher, a renowned expert in the realm of Qur'an and hadith scholarship and a walking encyclopedia of Islamic doctrinal issues.

7. **Ayatollah Āqā Ḥusayn Qumī**[4] a pious man and an expert in hadith scholarship who served as a high-ranking religious authority in Iran.

8. **Ayatollah 'Alī b. Ibrāhīm Qumī**[5] an eminent scholar in the fields of hadith scholarship and Islamic ethics.

9. **Ayatollah Muḥammad-'Alī Gharawī Urdūbādī**[6] a figure who had a long-lasting effect on the character and career of his disciples and colleagues. He was a logician,

1. d. 1365 AH/ 1945
2. d. 1961 AH/ 1942
3. d. 1373 AH/ 1953
4. d. 1366 AH/ 1946
5. d. 1373 AH/ 1953
6. d. 1380 AH/ 1960

philosopher, Qur'an and hadith interpreter, and renowned historian. His Arabic prose was regarded as exemplary, and he was a shining star in the constellation of Arabic literature.[1] In 1350 AH/1931, he issued a fifty-one-page diploma for Allāma Amīnī (then known as Sheikh 'Abd al-Ḥusayn), permitting him to relate and interpret hadiths. He would read and listen to *al-Ghadīr*, giving constructive suggestions with regard to stylisitc elegance.[2] Indeed, sometimes Allāma Amīnī would read the text of his *al-Ghadīr* to Ayatollah Urdūbādī himself; we can see the result of this partnership in the incredible success of the book.

10. **Ayatollah Āqā Buzurg (Muḥammad-Muḥsin) Ṭihrānī**[3] a famous author, and the compiler of the most comprehensive, twenty-five volume bibliography of Shia scholarship, *al-Dharī'ah ilā taṣānīf al-Shī'ah*. Besides his piety, he became distinguished for studying the bulk of Shia literature. His bibliography is to this day unrivalled. His *ijaza* for Sheikh 'Abd al-Ḥusayn was issued in 1353 AH/1934.

11. **Ayatollah Yaḥyā Khu'ī**[4] who studied in Tabriz and Khuy, a town in Northwest Iran. He migrated to Najaf and became a prominent figure in the field of jurisprudence, principles of jurisprudence, hadith, and Islamic history. There, he issued *ijazas* for relating hadiths to a number of scholars including Sheikh 'Abd al-Ḥusayn in 1380 AH/1960.

1. Allama Amīnī used to read out and check the text of his *al-Ghadīr* and its Arabic prose in front of Ayatollah Urdūbādī for its stylistic improvement. The result was superb: nobody has ever detected even a single mistake in the Arabic text of *al-Ghadīr*.

2. For his life sketch, see Muḥammad Alwānsāz Khu'ī, "Mirza Muḥammad-'Alī Urdūbādī," in *Gulshan-i abrār* (Qum, 1378 Sh/ 1999), vol. 4, pp. 417-424; and Grand Ayatollah Sayyid Mūsā Shubayrī-Zanjānī, *Jur'ah-yī az daryā* (Qum, 1389 Sh/ 2010), vol. 1, pp. 577-578.

3. d. 1389 AH/ 1969

4. d. 1364 AH/ 1944

12. **Ayatollah 'Abd al-Wāḥid Sarābī Tabrīzī Sardahā'ī Khīyābānī**[1] was a teacher of advanced levels of jurisprudence in Najaf before whom Allāma Amīnī used to receive at least fourteen lessons in both jurisprudence, issues in caliphate, and imamate roughly in the early 1350s AH/ 1931. This is evident from a manuscript of Allāma Amīnī, titled "Kitāb al-majālis" catalogued at the Imam Amīr al-Mu'minīn Public Library at Najaf.

Recitation of and attachment to the Holy Qur'an

Ayatollah Amīnī's personal schedule was such that he would recite one thirtieth of the Qur'an (*juz'*) every day, thereby completing a recitation of the entire Qur'an each month. In the month of Ramadan his recitation schedule was raised to a different level altogether, and he would complete a reading of the entire Qur'an every two days. With fifteen complete recitations every Ramadan and one complete recitation in each of the remaining eleven months, Ayatollah Amīnī's recitation schedule was such that he would recite the Qur'an twenty-six times in a year. With such extraordinary discipline, it is no surprise that Ayatollah Amīnī would achieve so much in scholarship.

1. d. unknown

Works Transcribed by Allāma Amīnī

Some of the works transcribed by Allāma Amīnī in the course of his research are still available in the public library he established in Najaf. They may be listed as follows. As extensive as the list is, it does not include the numerous books and treatises he transcribed on trips to India, Syria, Turkey, and Iran.

1. *Da'ā'im al-islām fī ma'rifah al-ḥalāl wa al-ḥarām wa al-qaḍāyā wa al-aḥkām al-ma'thūrah 'an Ahl al-Bayt* by Qāḍī al-Nu'mān b. Muḥammad b. Manṣūr b. Aḥmad al-Maghribī al-Miṣrī.[1]

2-3. *Kitāb al-amālī* and *al-Majālis* by Muḥammad b. Muḥammad b. al-Nu'mān al-Baghdādī "Sheikh al-Mufīd".[2]

4. *Kitāb al-mazār al-kabīr* by Abū 'Abd Allāh Muḥammad b. Ja'far b. 'Alī b. Ja'far al-Mashhadī al-Ḥā'irī.[3]

5. *Īḍāḥ al-dafā'in al-nawāṣib* by Abū al-Ḥasan Muḥammad b. Aḥmad b. 'Alī b. al-Ḥasan b. Shādhān al-Qummī.[4]

6-8. *Al-Ṭuraf; al-Yaqīn fī imrah Amīr al-Mu'minīn*; and *al-Anwār al-bāhirah fī intiṣār al-'itrah al-ṭāhirah* by Raḍī al-Dīn Abī al-Qāsim 'Alī b. Mūsā b. Ṭāwūs al-Ḥusaynī al-Ḥillī.[5]

1. d. 363 AH/ 973
2. d. 413 AH/ 1022
3. d. 6th/12th cent.
4. d. 6th/ 12th cent.
5. d. 664 AH/ 1265

9-13. *Nawādir al-athar fī anna 'Alīyyan khayr al-bashar; al-Akhbār al-musalsalāt; al-A'māl al-māni'ah min al-jannah; Jāmi' al-aḥādīth;* and *al-Ghāyāt* by Abū Muḥammad Ja'far b. Aḥmad b. 'Alī al-Qummī (resident of Rayy).[1]

14. *Khaṣā'is al-a'immah* by Abū al-Ḥasan Muḥammad b. al-Ḥusayn al-Mūsawī al-Baghdādī "al-Sharīf al-Raḍī".[2]

15. *Kitāb al-saqīfah* by Sulaym b. Qays al-Hilālī al-'Āmirī al-Kūfī.[3]

16. *Al-Ijāzah al-kabīrah li 'ulamā' al-Ḥuwayzah* by Sayyid 'Abd Allāh b. Nūr al-Dīn b. Ni'mat Allāh al-Jazā'irī.[4]

17. *Al-Masā'il al-arba'ūn al-kalāmīyyah* by Shahīd al-Awwal, Muḥammad b. Makkī al-'Āmilī.[5]

18-19. *Jazwah al-salām fī masā'il al-kalām* and *Jumal al-ādāb* by Sheikh Muḥammad Ṭāhir al-Samāwī.[6] The latter is a poetic version of a book by 'Īsā b. Dāb[7] which contains seventy merits of the immediate successor to Prophet Muḥammad and the first infallible, Imam 'Alī.

20. A book authored by al-Ḥusayn b. 'Uthmān b. Sharīk.

21. *Kitāb al-zuhd* by Ḥusayn b. Sa'īd al-Ahwāzī (3rd/ 9th cent.).

22. A book authored by Abī Sa'īd 'Abbād al-'Uṣfurī (2nd/ 8th cent.)[8]

---

1. d. 4th/10th cent.
2. d. 406 AH/ 1015
3. d. c. 90 AH/ 708
4. d. 786 AH/ 1384
5. martyred 786 AH/ 1384
6. d. 1370 AH/ 1950
7. d. 171 AH/ 787
8. It appears that earlier Muslim authors did not always name their

23. A book authored by Ja'far b. Muḥammad al-Haḍramī (2nd/ 8th cent.).

24. A book authored by Khallād al-Sindī (2nd/ 8th cent.).

25. A book authored by Zayd al-Nirsī (2nd/ 8th cent.).

26. A book authored by 'Abd Allāh b. Yaḥyā al-Kāhilī (2nd/ 8th cent.).

27. A book authored by 'Abd al-Mālik b. al-Ḥakīm (2nd/ 8th cent.).

28. A book authored by 'Āṣim b. Ḥumayd (2nd/ 8th cent.).

29. A book authored by Muthannā b. Walīd al-Ḥannāt (2nd/ 8th cent.).

30. A book authored by Muḥammad b. al-Muthannā al-Ḥaḍaramī (2nd/ 8th cent.).

31. *Mukhtaṣar aṣl* by 'Alā' b. Razīn (2nd/ 8th cent.).

32. *Masā'il* by 'Alī b. Ja'far (2nd/ 8th cent.).

33. *Al-Nawādir* by 'Alī b. Asbāt (2nd/8th cent.).

34. *Al-Arba'ūn hadīthan fī manāqib Amīr al-Mu'minīn 'alayh al-salām* by Ibn Abī al-Fawāris.

35. *Tazwīj Amīr al-Mu'minīn ibnatihi min 'Umar b. al-Khaṭṭāb* by al-Sharīf al-Murtaḍā.[1]

36. *Muqtaḍab al-athar* by Ibn 'Ayyāsh al-Jawharī.[2]

37. *Al-Mukhtaṣar min kitāb al-muwāfaqah li Ibn Sammān* by

---

books and that titling books and treatises was a later practice.

1. d. 436 AH/ 1044

2. d. 4th/10th cent.

al-Zamakhsharī.[1]

38. *Miftāḥ al-najā fī manāqib Āl al-'Abā* by al-Badakhshī.[2]

39. *Manāqib 'Alī b. Abī Ṭālib* by Ibn al-Maghāzilī.[3] [4]

40. A book authored by Durust b. Abī Manṣūr (2nd/ 8th cent.).

41. A book authored by Sallām b. Abī 'Umrah (2nd /8th cent.).

42. *Muṣādiqah al-ikhwān* by Sheikh al-Ṣadūq.[5]

43. *Al-Arba'ūn ḥadīthan* by Muḥy al-Dīn al-Ḥalabī.[6] [7]

44. *Al-Arba'ūn ḥadīthan* by Ḥusayn b. 'Abd al-Samad al-'Āmilī (10th/ 16th cent.).

45. *Al-Arba'ūn 'an al-arba'īn min al-arba'īn* by Sheikh Muntajab al-Dīn al-Rāzī.[8]

1. d. 539 AH/ 1144
2. d. 11th/17th cent.
3. d. 483 AH/ 109
4. This book has been published as *Manāqib al-Imām 'Alī b. Abī Ṭālib 'alayh al-salām*, ed. Muḥammad-Bāqir al-Bihbūdī (Beirut, 1403 AH/ 1983; 1424 AH/ 2003).
5. d. 381 AH/ 991
6. d. 6th/ 12th cent.
7. It has been a custom amongst Muslim religious scholars, on the basis of recommendations in Islamic teachings, to collect forty hadiths. It is, therefore, common to see books with *arba'een* (Arabic 'forty') in the title.
8. d. 6th/ 12th cent.

Allāma Amīnī's Other Works

In addition to transcribing works in pursuit of his research, Allāma Amīnī would also edit works. He had a special regard for pilgrimage (*zīārat*) texts, considered to be a much-neglected aspect of both practical devotion and religious scholarship. One of the valuable classics he collated, edited, and published was a highly reliable collection of salutations of the Prophet's household, *Kāmil al-zīārat*, by Ja'far b. Muḥammad b. Qūlawayh al-Qummī.[1] The book is devoted to detailing the etiquettes of various pilgrimages, and listing the salutations relating to them. The publishing of Allāma's version of the book in Najaf (1356 AH/ 1937) revived the popularity of *Kāmil al-zīārat.* The Arabic edition was published in Tehran, Qum, and Beirut, and it was translated into Persian, Urdu, and English.[2] Furthermore, the reintroduction of *Kāmil al-zīārat* prompted the publication of several other collections of pilgrimage texts, such as the seven volume of *Mawsū'ah zīārat al-ma'ṣūmīn.*[3]

Also relating to pilgrimage is Ayatollah Amīnī's *Adab al-*

1. d. 367 AH/ 977

2. There are currently at least two English translations, one by Sayyid Muḥsin al-Husaini al-Milani (published in Miami, 2008) and one by Sayyid Athar Husain S. H. Rizvi (published in Mumbai, 1431 AH/ 2010; repr. Karbala, 1434 AH/ 2013).

3. [Ayatollah Sayyid Hādī Rafī'īpūr 'Alawī (ed.)], *Mawsū'ah zīārat al-ma'ṣūmīn*, 7 vols., Qum, 1383 Sh/ 2004. This is a unique, well-researched, and carefully edited collection of the pilgrimage prayer-texts available for leading luminaries in the Islamic tradition, starting with Prophet Muḥammad and continuing with the infallible Imams and their various descendants. The work uses both Sunni and Shia sources. The Imam al-Hādī Research Institute in Qum has produced several other excellent collections which are worth consulting.

zā'īr liman yamamm al-ḥā'ir, a book exclusively concerned with the rituals associated with the pilgrimage of the third infallible, Imam al-Ḥusayn. Originally published in Najaf in 1362 AH/ 1943, and drawing upon a number of authoritative references, this compact and beautifully organized manual contains eighty rituals for the pilgrim and details recommended and non- recommended actions. Apparently, Allāma Amīnī was inspired to compile *Adab al-zā'ir* whilst editing *Kāmil al-ziārat*. His compilation of a book specifically on the proper ways of paying pilgrimage to Imam al-Ḥusayn attests to his special affection for and profound devotion to the Imam. The manual has also been translated into Persian.

From the Shia perspective, pilgrimage rituals are packed with meaning or religious spirit. Hence, they effectively reinforce the pilgrim's attention toward Allah and the love of the Prophet's household. The salutations recited during pilgrimage are full of educative lessons in religion and methods of how to become closer to Allah.

In the above-mentioned *Shuhadā' al-faḍīlah*, Ayatollah Amīnī puts forward a condensed biography of 130 martyred Shia clerics from the 4th/10th century through to his own time in the 14th/20th century. It is clear that this book deserves to be edited, updated, and translated.

Two reasons have been given as to why Allāma Amīnī chose to write the above work. The first possible reason is that he was motivated as a result of the execution of Ayatollah Sheikh Muḥammad Khīyābānī in Tabriz. At that time Allāma Amīnī was 18 years old. Ayatollah Khīyābānī was hung by pro-Russian communist Cossack forces on 29 Dhu al-Hijjah 1338 AH/ 13 September 1920. The second reason was that he wrote it as a response to the anti-Shia claims and accusations of the Egyptian author Aḥmad

Amīn. Rather than penning a direct rebuttal, Allāma Amīnī decided to illustrate the depth of Shia devotion and history.

Although written upon his return to Tabriz after his first stay in Najaf, *Shuhadā' al-faḍīlah* was published in Najaf in 1355 AH/ 1936 and was well received by the scholars of the city. This was a good choice as the printing-houses of Iran faced restrictions at the hands of the ruling authorities. However, in 1393 AH/ 1973, the book was published in Qum with endorsing forewords as well as a Persian translation.

Shuhadā' al-faḍīlah was a demonstration of Allāma Amīnī's rich scholarship and displayed his access to important records. The impact of his work was amazing and he received several letters of appreciation from Najaf, Baghdad, Tehran, and other cities of the Muslim world, including from Ayatollah Sayyid Abū al-Ḥasan Mūsawī Iṣfahānī,[1] Ayatollah Sayyid Ḥusayn Ṭabāṭabā'ī-Qumī,[2] and Ayatollah Muḥammad-Ḥusayn Gharawī Iṣfahānī.[3] It was not only clerics who were impressed by the work; Allāma also received praise of the work from Dr. Tawfīq al-Fukaykī of Baghdad.[4]

The enthusiastic reception of *Shuhadā' al-faḍīlah* encouraged Allāma Amīnī to write another biography, "Rijāl-i Ādharbāyijān" which focuses on 234 scholars from his home region. Through such works, Allāma Amīnī conveyed

1. d. 1365 AH/ 1945

2. d. 1366 AH/ 1946

3. d. 1361 AH/ 1942

4. For further information on *Shuhadā' al-faḍīlah* see Ayatollah Sayyid Mūsā Shubayrī-Zanjānī, *Jur'ah-yī az daryā* (Qum, 1390 Sh/ 2012), vol. 2, pp. 604-606. Ayatollah Allama Sayyid Muḥammad-Ṣādiq Baḥr al-'Ulūm also commented on the work, as indicated in al-Ḥillī, *Fihris maktabah al-'Allāma al-Sayyid Muḥammad-Ṣādiq Baḥr al-'Ulūm* (Qum, 1431 AH/ 1389 Sh/ 2010), p. 310, no. 347.

the importance he placed on history and showed that his interests spanned further than matters relating to purely Islamic religious doctrines.

Allāma Amīnī had a historical outlook in his works. Although he is largely recognized as a theologian and hadith scholar, he developed his own view of history, too. According to Allāma, there are at least two types of history: "narrative" (common) vs. "true" (analytical) history. While the former is simply a narrative or mere report of certain outstanding events that took place in the past, the latter focuses on the background, context, and the real causes of why certain events took place. An example of "narrative history" is *Shuhadā' al-faḍīlah*; *al-Ghadīr* is a prototype of "true" (analytical) history. While both types of history have their own uses and utilities, it is the second type that proves insightful, thought-provoking, and didactic. Allāma Amīnī applied his analytical historical framework to the development of certain doctrinal terminologies, for he believed that major digressions in Islamic history can be disclosed and fully understood only in the light of appreciating the factual backgrounds and contexts of what befell Islamic history.

Another work stemming from Allāma Amīnī's interlude in Tabriz include *Tafsīr fātiḥat al-kitāb*, which was posthumously published in Arabic in Tehran (1395 AH/ 1975) and also later published in Persian. This interpretation of the opening *sura* (chapter) of the Qur'an is split into two main sections. The first section provides its interpretation, while the second section discusses some conceptual matters which arise in his discussion of the Fātiḥa, such as certain key points, such as the unicity of Allah, free will and determination. This Qur'an interpretation is flavoured by Allāma Amīnī's reliance exclusively on the authoritative exegetical hadiths related from the Infallible Imams, with special regard to the key concept of the authority (*wilāyah*) of the Infallible Imams. It was the late Ayatollah Riḍā Amīnī who edited and published the work in Tehran. The first part of this Qur'an interpretation focuses on the sura in question. The following topics are dealt with: other variant names (titles) of the sura; comprehensiveness of this sura with regard to the Qur'anic fields of scholarship; the shared areas between this sura and other suras of the Qur'an; some miraculous effects and virtues of this sura; and some moral lessons deducible from it. The second part is devoted to the Islamic doctrinal and philosophical points derivable from the verses of this sura, including characteristics of Allah, the Divine determination and man's free will, the Divine eternal fate, and so forth. In doing so, only the exegetical hadiths of Prophet Muḥammad and other Infallible Imams are drawn upon.

The late Ayatollah Riḍā Amīnī added two further parts to the Persian translation of the book accomplished by Qudrat Allāh Ḥusaynī Shāhmurādī, a Tehran-based retired high school teacher of mathematics and geometry who used to be both a disciple and a companion of Allāma Amīnī. In this third part, some further points are added as extended end-notes to the doctrinal points highlighted in the previous two parts. There is a fourth part that deals with an over-view of a Qur'an interpretation ascribed to the eleventh Infallible Imam al-Ḥasan al-'Askarī (232-260 AH/ 845-872); the book of religious beliefs derived from the statements of the eighth Infallible Imam 'Alī al-Riḍā (148-203 AH/ 765-817); and the topic of the eternal and accidental modes of fate. In all these discussions, a hadith backed and ethically oriented approach is evident throughout.

In 1384 AH/ 1964, Allāma Amīnī took a research trip to

Syria which lasted four months. Of this, he spent 22 days in Aleppo where he was uncovering resources in places such as the provincial branch of the Syrian National Library for his book on the event of Ghadīr. During his stay in Aleppo he met Sheikh Muḥammad Sa'īd Daḥdūḥ, an important and leading cleric of the region, with whom he became good friends. He also met other Sunnis of Aleppo and was faced with their queries on Shia beliefs.

As he continued his research for his compendium on the event of Ghadīr, Allāma Amīnī also addressed some concerns from the Sunni School in the book *Sīratunā wa sunnatunā sīrah nabīyyinā wa sunnatih*, published in Najaf in 1384 AH/1965. The book was organized into three sections. The first section deals with having ardent love of the Prophet and his Infallible household. In it, he asserts that sincere devotion to them cannot be considered as excess or exaggeration. The second and largest section of the volume deals with the commemoration of the events of Karbala in Muharram, and the tragic, yet triumphant, martyrdom of Imam al-Ḥusayn and his companions. Allāma Amīnī draws upon authentic hadiths from Sunni sources which indicate that Prophet Muḥammad was in fact the first dignitary in Islam who shed tears for the martyrdom of Imam al-Ḥusayn at his birth. Indeed, the hadith corpus suggests that the Prophet mourned the martyrdom of Imam al-Ḥusayn on twenty-four different occasions, both at home and in public. In this way Allāma explains that Shias follow the Prophetic practice in their Muharram commemorations.

In the third and final section, Allāma Amīnī demonstrates that the Shia practice of prostrating on earth during prayer originates from the customs which are based entirely on Prophet Muḥammad and his close companions who, according to Sunni hadith resources used to prostrate on pieces of stone or the earth.[1]

In addition to his *Tafsīr fātiḥat al-kitāb*, further works by Ayatollah Amīnī were published posthumously. The first was another exegesis, discussing the primordial (pre-creation) world of pre-existence (*'ālam al-dhar*) through an exploration of four verses of the Qur'an and relevant hadiths. *Al-Maqāṣid al-'āliyyah fī al-maṭālib al-sanīyyah*, edited by Sayyid Muḥammad Ṭabāṭabā'ī Yazdī, was published in Qum in 1434 AH/ 2013.

Thamarāt al-asfār ilā al-aqṭār, another posthumously published work, was originally written in two volumes, the first is a record of some of the fine manuscripts Allāma encountered during his research expeditions in prominent libraries of India in 1380 AH/ 1960. The second volume pertains to some of his important discoveries during his four-month research trip to Syria. The book was later published in four volumes in Qum in 1428-29 AH/ 2007-08.

There are also several works by Allāma Amīnī which remain in manuscript form, and have yet to be published. In a two-volume work, titled *Rīyāḍ al-uns*, the first 700-page volume collects Arabic and Persian literary pieces, and the second 1012-page volume is a research diary recorded during his compilation of *al-Ghadīr*.

1. *Sīratunā wa sunnatunā sīrah nabīyyinā wa sunnatih* was translated into Persian as *Rāh wa rawishva ravish-i mā rāh wa ravish-i Piyāmbar-i mā-ast* (Tehran, 1388 AH/ 1968; 1394 AH/ 1974) by Ayatollah Sayyid Muḥammad-Bāqir Mūsawī Hamidānī (d. 1379 Sh/ 1421 AH/ 2000). The translation was assessed by Allama Amīnī; as an example of his diligence we can see that he has added new points in certain places, e.g., p. 261, n. 1, and p. 262, n. 1.

I'ām al-anām fī ma'rifah al-Malik al-'Allām is a work concerned with teaching people the conception of Islamic monotheism (*tawḥīd*). Despite its Arabic title, the work was written in Persian. From the Safavid period until the mid-twentieth century, it was common and somewhat prestigious for Islamic religious texts published in Iran to bear Arabic titles.

Another unpublished work discusses the significance of pilgrimage (*ziyara*), and was written in response to some queries Allāma Amīnī had received from some scholars from Pakistan. Furthermore, there is an unpublished work of Qur'an interpretation, "al-'Itrah al-ṭāhirah fī al-kitāb al-'Azīz" which analyses Qur'anic verses pertaining to the merits of the Prophet and his infallible descendants.

Allāma Amīnī also produced several commentaries on books in jurisprudence, including the *Farā'id al-uṣūl* and *Makāsib* of Sheikh Murtaḍā Anṣārī[1], the renowned and influential Najaf-based, Iranian jurisprudent (*faqih*).

1. d. 1281 AH/ 1864

PART TWO

AUTHORING AL-GHADĪR

"When you hear a narration,
think of putting it into practice
and not with the reasoning of just
narrating it, for verily the narrators
of knowledge are many and those
who attend to it are few."

- IMAM ʻALĪ

Why Ghadīr?

The work Allāma Amīnī is most well-known for, his magnum opus, is *al-Ghadīr*. This voluminous book, written in Arabic, offers an in-depth analysis of major events which took place in the Muslim community shortly after the death of Prophet Muḥammad.

It is said that the idea for writing *al-Ghadīr* came about when Allāma Amīnī returned to Najaf to study for the second time. In search of a direction for his scholarly career, Allāma Amīnī paid a visit to the shrine of Imam ʻAlī. It was after this pilgrimage that he became inspired to critically examine the historical documents that pertain to the right of Imam ʻAlī. His focal point was the event of Ghadīr Khumm which he believed to be the backbone of Islam; an event whose immense significance was both political and religious. Using the example of Ghadīr, he would go on to prove one of the most fundamental ideological and political principles of Shiism: "Immate and Authority".

A Brief History

The Distinctions of ʻAlī ibn Abī Ṭālib from a Young Age

During the introduction of Islam in seventh century Arabia, Prophet Muḥammad had two loyal followers: his wife, Khadījah, and his paternal cousin, Imam ʻAlī. Imam ʻAlī's closeness to Prophet Muḥammad was unmistakable; in addition to being raised almost entirely by him, Imam ʻAlī was present for most key events in the Prophet's life. Long before revelation, even during the Prophet's month-long retreats, Imam ʻAlī would take meals to him at the end of his fast. He was also present at the first Divine revelation in the Cave of Ḥirā (Mecca, on the evening of 27 Rajab 13 BH). Imam ʻAlī was, from the start, a true believer and unlike the other inhabitants of Mecca who adored and worshipped idols, Imam ʻAlī never cast any doubt on the prophethood or Divine mission of Moḥammad.

Prophet Muḥammad often highlighted the merits of Imam ʻAlī to the people in preparation for making and introducing him as his immediate successor. All the major prophets (*ulu al-ʻaẓm*) nominated deputies and successors, both for the administration of their own affairs, and the continuation of their prophetic missions. Moses had made Aaron his successor; Jesus Christ had his twelve apostles, and Prophet Muḥammad nominated ʻAlī.

Daʻwah al-ʻAshīrah

In the third year after the declaration of prophethood, Prophet Muḥammad was instructed to invite his own tribe to Islam so he asked Imam 'Alī to invite forty men from his tribe of Quraysh. The Prophet informed them of his prophetic mission. Then he asked: "Now, who is there among you to help me in this mission so that he shall become my successor?" From all in attendance, only Imam 'Alī stood up to say "I shall help you."

The Prophet repeated the question three times. Each time, no one responded except Imam 'Alī. Finally, the Prophet turned to 'Alī and addressed him by saying: "You shall be my successor after me."

Protecting the Prophet

The Year of Grief (*'ām al-ḥuzn*) occurred ten years later. It was named thus because the Prophet suffered the death of both his first wife, Khadījah, and his paternal uncle Abū Ṭālib in the same year. Khadījah had supported Islam not only through her words as the first lady to accept the religion, but also through the devotion of all her abundant wealth and commercial influence to support her husband's prophetic mission.

The Prophet's loss of these two pillars of support caused the pagans of Mecca to erroneously feel emboldened, and free to plot the assassination of the Prophet in order to put an end to Islam. Through revelation, the Prophet became aware of their plot and began taking the necessary precautions.

On the night that the assassins came to the bed of the Prophet, they lifted the covers to kill him, only to find to their surprise, Imam 'Alī in the Prophet's bed. Having risked his life to act as a decoy, Imam 'Alī's inimitable sacrifice received Divine approval in the Qur'an (see Sura al-Baqarah

2: 207). It was this selflessness on the part of the Imam that allowed the Prophet to make his way to Medina in a migration (*hijrah*) so significant that it now marks the beginning of the Islamic calendar.

There are many instances recorded in books of hadith which illustrate Imam 'Alī's courage, strength of character, and unerring support for Islam and the Holy Prophet. The Holy Qur'an itself pays testament to Imam 'Alī's virtue; Sura al-Mā'idah, verse 55, tells of the time Imam 'Alī gave his ring as an act of charity during prayer, and Sura al-Aḥzāb verse 33, reports the event of Hadith al-Kisā'. Stories from the battlefield, including the legendary accounts of the Battles of Badr and Khaybar, are found scattered in every major hadith document; all of which acknowledge Imam 'Alī's strength and bravery.

The History of Ghadīr

In Classical Arabic, the word "*ghadīr*" means "place in a desert where a pool is left by the rain." Ghadīr Khumm is located near a place called Juḥfah between Mecca and Madina. Some of the tribes used to wash their dyed clothes there and it was like the barrel of diers and, it became known as "Khumm".

In the tenth year of Hijra, the Prophet travelled from Medina to Mecca to perform a pilgrimage. News of his journey had reached Muslims from numerous regions. They began to gather in Mecca in order to be in the company of the Prophet and perform the rituals of the pilgrimage according to his practices.

During the rituals, the Prophet delivered several speeches to the people. After the hajj ceremonies, he decided to return to Medina. On his journey back, accompanied by the crowds who continued to follow him, the Prophet reached the hilly spot of Juḥfah, also known as Ghadīr Khumm. It was here that the Archangel of Revelation, Gabriel, descended upon the Prophet with this verse of the Holy Qur'an:

"O Messenger! Proclaim what descended to you from your Lord; and if you do not do so, you have not proclaimed His message, and Allah protects you from the people."
(Sura al-Mā'idah 5: 67)

The Prophet acted without hesitation. After the noon prayers, he gave the order to have a pulpit (*minbar*) made; this was done so by heaping multiple camels' saddles on top of each other. According to a number of reliable historians, the gathering around the pulpit that day consisted of 120,000 people. The Prophet stood on the pulpit. Every sign indicated that the matter he was to speak of was of great importance; the Prophet had stopped in the middle of a hot desert rather than seeking the ease and the comfort of a town. The people were anxious to know why the matter was of such significance.

Prophet Muḥammad predicted the nearness of his death, which he had also done in Mecca. He said:

"It seems the time has approached when I shall be called away (by Allah) and I shall answer that call. I am leaving for you two precious things and if you adhere to them both, you will never go astray after me. They are the Book of Allah and my Progeny, that is my Ahl al-Bayt. The two shall never separate from each other until they come to me by the Pool (of Paradise)."

This saying is widely known as "*hadith al-thaqalayn*", which means "the tradition of the two weighty things". The Messenger of Allah continued to say:

"Do I not have more right over the believers than what they have over themselves?"

The people unanimously answered:
"Yes, O Messenger of Allah!"

He spoke of his Prophethood, and that he was acting on the will of Allah in announcing the Divine revelations to the people. He then declared that he had one last announcement, which would complete the religion. After these words, he called 'Alī b. Abī Ṭālib. Imam 'Alī went next to him on the *minbar*. The Prophet took his hand and lifted it above his head so that, as historians have indicated, the whiteness of their armpits showed.

There, in the searing-hot desert, holding Imam 'Alī's hand high above his head, stopping all passing caravans, the Holy Prophet declared:

"For whomever I am his Leader (*mawlā*), 'Alī is his Leader (*mawlā*). O Allah! May You love those who love him, and be hostile to those who are hostile to him."

In this way, the Prophet blessed those who would help 'Alī and cursed those who would refrain from helping him.

Through this splendid ceremony, the Prophet officially introduced and nominated Imam 'Alī to be his immediate successor. Immediately after the Prophet finished his speech, the following Qur'anic verse was revealed in appreciation:

"Today I have perfected your religion and completed my favour upon you, and I was satisfied that Islam be your religion." (Sura al-Mā'idah 5:3)

Without settling the significant matter of leadership after the Prophet, Islam would never reach perfection. It follows that completion of the Islamic religion was surely as a direct result of the introduction and announcement of the Prophet's immediate successor.

People from the gathering approached Imam 'Alī one after the other congratulating, him, and kissing his hand as a token of their allegiance to him. Among those who did so was 'Umar b. al-Khaṭṭāb, who said:

"Well done Ibn Abī Ṭālib! Today you have become the Leader (*mawlā*) of all believing men and women."

Lastly, Prophet Muḥammad conferred the honorific title of 'Amīr al Mu'minīn', 'The Prince of the Faithful' on Imam 'Alī and ordered all people to congratulate and refer to him by his new and specific title. In this way, people expressed their approval and support. According to some historians, the Prophet remained three days and nights at Ghadīr Khumm so that all the people could pledge allegiance.

At the request of Prophet Muḥammad, the event of Ghadīr Khumm was marked by a poem composed and recited by Ḥassān b. Thābit[1] immediately. This was in accordance with an Arab custom that any significant event, whether joyous or tragic, becomes permanent in the memory of people through poetry. Today, the many poems that relate to the event of Ghadīr Khumm, such as the one quoted below, comprise an important genre of the Islamic literary tradition.

1. d. 40 AH/ 660

Their Prophet calls them, (on the day of Ghadīr)
At Khumm so hear and heed the Messenger's call,
He said: "Who is your guide and leader?
(*mawlākum wa walīyyukum*)"
They said, and there was no apparent blindness (clearly):
"Your God, our guide, and you are our leader
And you won't find from among us,
in this, any disobedient,"
He said to him: "Stand up O 'Alī, for I am
Pleased to announce you Imam and guide after me
(*min ba'dī imām(an) wa hādīy(an)*),
So whomever I was his leader (*mawlā*),
then this is his leader (*mawlā*)
So be to him supporters in truth and followers,"
There he prayed: "O Allah! Be a friend and guide to his
follower and be, to the one who is 'Alī's enemy, an enemy."

After the Holy Prophet Left this World

After the death of the Holy Prophet, a gathering met in Saqīfah Banī Sā'idah, contrary to the clear indications and directives of Prophet Muḥammad. They decided that Abū Bakr should succeed the Prophet and govern the Muslims instead of Imam 'Alī. This led to a series of events which proved to be very damaging to the legacy of Islam, and particularly to the household of the Prophet. These bitter events, which occurred within the first three months after the death of the Prophet included: the raid on the house of Imam 'Alī, the death of his unborn son, Muḥsin, the fatal injury to his wife Lady Fāṭimah al-Zahrā, (daughter of the Prophet), and the usurpation and confiscation of Fadak, a fertile region which the Prophet had gifted to Lady Fāṭimah al-Zahrā.

A further oppression was the official prevention of the relation, narration, and transcription of prophetic hadiths in favour of the Prophet's Infallibe household. Abū Bakr issued an order that no words of Prophet Muḥammad should be related, and if you are asked a question, you should know that the Book of Allah, the Qur'an, is sufficient for you, and you should do just as the Qur'an says. This declaration was enforced in a directive sent to all Muslim territories, where Abū Bakr said that all transcriptions of the words of Prophet Muḥammad must be destroyed. He also strictly warned all hadith recorders, including the companions of Prophet Muḥammad, against the narration, dissemination, and transcription of Prophetic hadiths.

In response, Imam 'Alī decided to act in the best interests of Islamic unity by not beginning an uprising against those who did not follow for this would have split the Ummah. He preferred maintaining the Prophet's instructions at Ghadīr and chose to forsake his rights and transitory interests for the longevity of Islam.

After the death of Abū Bakr, Imam 'Alī's right continued to be ignored, and the caliphate was instead given to 'Umar b. al-Khaṭṭāb. Then, as the time of 'Umar's death approached, he called a *shūrā* (consultation board) to determine the next caliph. The *shūrā* chose 'Uthmān b. 'Affān to be the third caliph. In the Council of Six, after 'Uthmān was nominated and selected by 'Abd al-Raḥmān b. 'Awf, Imam 'Alī showed and explained his protest as well as his readiness for co-operation in the following words in *Nahj al-Balāghah*:

> You yourselves know that I have more merit for the office of caliphate than all others. And now I swear to Allah that as long as the affairs of the Muslims are in order, and

> my rivals are content with leaving me aside and only I am being treated unfairly, I will show no opposition and will submit. (*Nahj al-Balāghah,* Sermon 72)

It was only after the murder of 'Uthmān, 24 years later in 35 AH/ 656, after Ghadīr Khumm, that Imam 'Alī was asked to be the caliph and lead the Muslims. In one of his letters to Mālik al-Ashtar he wrote:

> At first, I withdrew my hand until I saw that some people turned back from Islam, and invited men to annihilate the religion of Muḥammad. I feared then that if I did not rise to aid Islam and Muslims, I would witness a split or destruction in Islam the calamity of which would be far greater than foregoing a short period of caliphate. (Letter 62 of *Nahj al-Balāghah*)

The brief history presented above charts the events which inspired Allāma Amīnī to write his book. He dedicated his life to the truth of Imam 'Alī's instructions and the following section is an attempt to portray how he was able to accomplish this.

A Son's Reflections on his Father's Success

When Allāma Amīnī's son, Sheikh Aḥmad Amīnī, was asked for the reasons behind his father's determination and drive, which enabled him to complete such an epic piece of work, he replied by listing three main factors. Firstly, Allāma was brought up in a religious environment; his father was a religiously devout scholar and his mother always took care to make the environment at home conducive to spirituality; therefore, from a young age he was familiar with the sights and sounds of Islam. Secondly, Allāma reached Najaf at a time of much enthusiasm for research and studying. He had good friends to discuss and consult with; they exerted a profound impact on his work. Thirdly, and most importantly, the more Allāma researched into the life of Imam 'Alī, the more attached he became to him. He loved the Imam more than anybody else, and this love gave him the energy, enthusiasm, and motivation which allowed him to accomplish great tasks.

Shiekh Aḥmad went on to remark thus: "He gave his life to Imam 'Alī. He saw himself as a sacrifice for the Imam. He did not see anything as important as serving Imam 'Alī. In fact, in his will to his own children, he instructed that they must continue to serve Imam 'Alī. It is evident that the fire that burned in his heart was not ignited by books, although the knowledge he had in this respect greatly helped him. Allāma had a great gift which one could only achieve as a token of kindness from Allah; to know a heart worthy of great love."

Allāma Amīnī's Aims Behind al-Ghadīr

A Sign of his Devotion to Imam 'Alī

Allāma Amīnī had great love for Imam 'Alī, which only intensified the more he researched his life. One of Allāma Amīnī's students recalls that he would often weep profusely over the oppression Imam 'Alī faced, as he read through various texts. Allāma Amīnī would regularly visit the shrine of Imam 'Alī when he faced difficulties in his research or could not find any book he needed; on many occasions his appeals to Imām 'Alī for help were immediately answered.

Islamic Unity

The appointment of Imam 'Alī at Ghadīr Khumm and the series of events that followed (as detailed above) have historically been a point of contention between Sunni and Shia Muslims. Through proving the existence and importance of Ghadīr, Allāma Amīnī actually intended to unite rather than divide the Muslim communities. This was an aim so close to the heart of Imam 'Alī himself that it formed the motivation behind many of his deeds following the death of the Holy Prophet. It only seems befitting that a man who dedicated his life to the service of Imam 'Alī would have such a high aim for his own book. In the preface to the first volume of his book, he makes a brief reference to the role that *al-Ghadīr* would have in the Muslim World, when he remarks:

> We consider all this a service to the (Islamic) religion, to elevate the 'truth', and revive the revival the original and ideal Islamic community.

In the preface to volume 5 of *al-Ghadīr*, Allāma Amīnī clearly explains his view on unity. In a section entitled "A Generous Opinion", he discusses a letter of appreciation he received about *al-Ghadīr* from Egypt. Here, Allāma Amīnī leaves no room for doubt.

> People are free to express their views and ideas on religion. These (views and ideas) will never tear apart the bond of Islamic fraternity to which the Holy Qur'an has referred by stating that "surely the believers are brethren" (Sura al-Ḥujurāt 49:10), even though academic discussions as well as theological and religious debates reach a peak. Notwithstanding, all the differences that we have in the primary and secondary principles, we, the compilers and writers, in nooks and corners of the world of Islam, share a common point and that is the very belief in the Almighty and His Prophet. A single spirit and one (form of) sentiment exists in all our bodies and souls, and that is the spirit of Islam and what we term 'sincerity'. We, the Muslim authors, live under the banner of truth and carry out our duties under the guidance of the Qur'an and the Prophetic mission of the Holy Prophet. The message of all of us is "Surely the (true) religion with Allah is Islam." (Āl 'Imrān 3:18) and our slogan is "There exists no other deity save Allah and Muḥammad is His Messenger." Indeed, we are (the members of) the party of Allah and the supporters of his religion (Ibid, Vol. 5, Preface).

Furthermore, the preface to volume 8 is entitled "*Al-Ghadīr* unites the ranks of the Muslim peoples." In this way, Allāma Amīnī enters into a direct discussion regarding the role of *al-Ghadīr* in Islamic unity. He strongly refutes the charges of those who say the event at Ghadīr causes a greater dispersion of Muslims, and argues that, on the contrary, *al-Ghadīr* removes many misunderstandings, thus bringing Muslims closer together. As evidence of this claim, he offers the statements of a number of Muslim scholars in support of this.

In fact, a large group of Sunni scholars endorsed Allāma Amīnī after having learned about *al-Ghadīr*. The Egyptian writer Muḥammad 'Abd al-Ghanī Ḥasan wrote in a plaque of honor forwarded to Allāma Amīnī,

> God willing, your clear water pool (*Ghadīr*) will serve as the cause of establishment of peace and friendship between Shia and Sunni brothers, so that they would unite to found the united Muslim nation (Ḥakīmī, 1998).

'Ādil Ghaḍbān, director of the Egyptian journal *Kitāb* said:

> The book *al-Ghadīr* clarifies all the rationale behind Shiism so Sunnis can use it to obtain an accurate knowledge of Shiism. Such accurate knowledge of Shiism can cause proximity between opinions of Shias and Sunnis so that Shias and Sunnis could form a united front.

Allāma Amīnī's Method

Sources

According to the account of the late Ayatollah Riḍā Amīnī, throughout the 40 years that Allāma Amīnī spent on the *al-Ghadīr* project, he devoted around 19 hours a day to working on the book.[1] Once Allāma Amīnī himself remarked that he had studied an average of 30,000 books to develop *al-Ghadīr* and he studied at least 200 pages for writing any page of his book.

Among the hadiths assessed in *al-Ghadīr*, the Prophet's sermon at Ghadīr Khumm features prominently. In the terminology of hadith studies, this sermon has the status of a *mutawātir* hadith, meaning that it has been repeated and related in many sources; its authenticity is therefore undeniable. Even the opponents of Imam 'Alī admit to its authenticity. Allāma Amīnī pieced together all the various texts of the Prophet's sermon at Ghadīr Khumm and listed all the people involved in relating it. Among the hadith relators, there are 110 companions of the Prophet, 84 *tābi'ūn* (followers of the companions), and 360 notable religious scholars. The sermon has been discussed by 26 authors, and the authenticity of the text has been confirmed by 43 prominent Sunni hadith scholars.

When it came to choosing the sources to underpin his research, Allāma Amīnī took a unique approach. In order to make his book credible to the whole Muslim community (*ummah*) and fulfill his aim of Islamic unity, Allāma decided to use only the reliable sources that were acceptable to the

1. *Risālat* [Tehran], (12 Tīr 1367 Sh/ 3 July 1998), p. 24.

Sunni school of thought and used Shia sources in specific cases, where use of them was necessary. Allāma Amīnī believed that Sunni sources must be used to prove the righteousness of the Ahl al-Bayt, especially Imam 'Alī, and always remained faithful to this principle belief in his work. For this purpose, he drew upon around 20,000 credible Sunni books, written and published across the centuries. Allāma Amīnī said, "*Al-Ghadīr* covers Islamic discussions, rather than specifically Shia discussions, thus, the sources invoked in this book are acceptable to all branches of Islam, rather than being only acceptable to Shias." He emphasized, "Shias invoke Sunni hadiths when debating with Sunnis, because Sunni hadiths are more acceptable to Sunnis.[1] "

Allāma Amīnī said, "I have mentioned the names of tens of Sunni hadith scholars who all have testified that the Hadith al-Ghadīr is both frequently cited (*mutawātir*) and certain (*maqṭū'*)." For example, Shams al-Dīn al-Dhahabī al-Shāfi'ī said, "This hadith is *mutawātir* and I am sure that the Prophetic hadith 'Of whomsoever I had been Master (*mawlā*), 'Alī here is to be his Master,' is indeed the very words of Prophet Muḥammad." As for the Hadith al-Ghadīr being *mutawātir*, Allāma Ḍīya' al-Dīn al-Muqbilī also wrote "If the Hadith al-Ghadīr is not indisputable, then nothing about Islam would be indisputable". Some Sunni scholars even wrote books on the subject; for example, Shams al-Dīn al-Shāf'ī wrote a book titled *Asnā al-maṭālib*, in which he demonstrated that the Hadith al-Ghadīr was *mutawātir* by invoking eighty chains of narrators for this hadith.[2]

In his assessment of the chain of narrators of the Hadith al-Ghadīr, Allāma Amīnī mentioned 110 prominent com-

1. Cited in 'Alīyābādī, 2010
2. Ibid.

panions (people who have visited Prophet Muḥammad). He expands on this, saying:

> Naturally, the number of narrators of this hadith must be several times as many as 110, because the number of companions who heard and recorded this hadith and narrated it to others after returning back home must have been hundreds of thousands, because passengers usually narrate to others the major events they have witnessed during their journey. (Allāma Amīnī, 1982).

In *al-Ghadīr*, the names of 84 of the followers (*tābi'ūn*) (people who never visited Prophet Muḥammad but visited his companions) who related the Hadith al-Ghadīr are mentioned.[1] Along with it, 360 scholars from the 2nd-4th /8th -10th centuries who quoted the Hadith Ghadīr with various chains of narrators. Allāma Amīnī was so concerned about this hadith that in addition to referring to these chains of relaters in his book, he included references to other authors who had referred to chains of narrators of this hadith in their books; a total of 36 persons.[2]

Allāma Amīnī was very meticulous when quoting materials from the original texts. He quoted from authoritative Sunni sources with utmost scholarly care and fidelity, and without the slightest alteration, and then, having provided the statement of a problem or misconception, he drew on quotations for the purpose of his arguments. The accuracy and fidelity with which he quoted sources earned him the title "*Amīn-i Naql*" "trustworthy". For instance, to prove the authority of Imam 'Alī, Allāma used Sunni sources and quoted personalities such as 'Umar b. al-Khaṭṭāb who said, "Prophet Muḥammad appointed 'Alī as the sign and guide"

1. Ibid., pp. 145-166
2. Ibid., p. 183

(cited by the Sunni hadith scholar and historian al-Qundūzī al-Ḥanafī). Allāma also quoted the following hadith from the Prophet from a number of Sunni sources: "Indeed, 'Alī is from me and I am from him, and he is the authority for every believer after me".

Allāma Amīnī created a global work, which transcended barriers of ethnicity and nationality, and belongs to the whole and greater community. Arab Christian scholars like Yusuf As'ad Dāghir and Boulos Salameh, paid attention to *al-Ghadīr*, and forwarded a plaque of honor to Allāma Amīnī for writing this book. It read "*Al-Ghadīr*, belongs to those who seek well-being in both worlds by following the teachings of the Qur'an, the Ahl al-Bayt and the Divine."

Allāma Amīnī believed that by inviting Sunnis to read his book it could help to reduce differences and tensions between branches of Islam, as each branch seeks to understand each the other. Writing a book which clearly and objectively outlines the beliefs of Shia Muslims was of utmost importance to Allāma's mission. As he observed:

> Like any Muslim, I find myself obliged to reduce differences, hostility, and hatred; however, one must figure out how this task can be accomplished. Many differences between Muslims result from the fact that they do not have an accurate understanding of the beliefs of one another. During the past centuries, and even in this century, many false things have been written about Shias, which have been used as a basis of judgement. (Cited in Ḥakīmī, 1998; cited in Ḥiydarī Abharī, *Bā Ghadīr wa al-Ghadīr*, in the form of a hypothetical dialogue with Allāma Amīnī).

The Quest for Resources

Allāma Amīnī gained a great reputation for locating rare books and fine manuscripts for his research, some of which required long journeys to different countries and cities (see the chapter on Allāma's travels). On a few occasions, he was unable to locate a work required for his research, despite exhausting his lines of enquiry through teachers and colleagues. On these occasions, he visited the shrine of Imam 'Alī (as well as that of Imam al-Ḥusayn), praying to Allah by His eminence, and by the eminence of the awaited Imam al-Mahdī. His prayers were often immediately granted.

A Treasure in the Wrapping!

Hajj Sayyid Kāẓim Mūsawī Khalkhālī, the son of a brother-in-law of Allāma Amīnī, told the present author that Allāma Amīnī had once noticed a precious book relevant to his *al-Ghadīr* project at a private library in India. However, the owner of the library refused to give him access to it. Several years passed by, and Allāma still longed for it. One day, he went to Imam 'Alī's Sacred Sanctuary to perform pilgrimage, and he prayed that he would obtain the book. On the way back home, he paused at a shop to buy some food, and he noticed that the shopkeeper intended to tear off a page of an old manuscript to wrap the item he had bought. Glancing at the paper, Allāma Amīnī found that the manuscript was exactly the very same one he had been searching for! Deeply amazed to have found it there, he offered the shopkeeper some money to purchase it. As the shopkeeper was unaware of the true research value of the book, he gave it to Allāma for free!

You will Never See This Book!

On another occasion, Allāma Amīnī was in need of the book *al-Ṣirāṭ al-mustaqīm ilā mustaḥaqqīyy al-taqdīm* by Sheikh Zayn al-Dīn Abū Muḥammad 'Alī b. Yūnus al-'Āmilī - a manuscript which was only available from a particular book collector in Najaf. He found the man and asked to borrow the book, but his request was purposely denied. Allāma Amīnī insisted for a few hours, but the man gave him the same answer, "You will never see this book!" Profoundly saddened, Allāma Amīnī went to the Sacred Sanctuary of Imam 'Alī to appeal for help. The next day, he took an urgent and short trip to Karbala; he felt the need to ask Imam al-Ḥusayn to help him obtain the book he needed. Allāma had barely completed the recommended rituals at Imam al-Ḥusayn's Sacred Sanctuary when one of the renowned Shia preachers of Karbala, named Sheikh Muḥsin Abū al-Ḥabb approached him and invited Allāma to his house.

While Allāma Amīnī was in the house of the Sheikh, one of the neighbours knocked at the door. The man had brought three manuscripts that had belonged to his late father. Since his children could not use the books, one of them decided to donate them to Sheikh Abū al-Ḥabb, knowing he was a learned figure in Karbala. When the package was opened, the book on the top of the pile was a transcript of the same book that Allāma had been searching for. Upon finding it in front of himself so unexpectedly, Allāma Amīnī burst into tears. Shortly after, Sheikh Abū al-Ḥabb donated the volume to Allāma Amīnī so he may use it to develop *al-Ghadīr*.

Al-Ālūsī's Library in Baghdad

There is a story of a famous Sunni scholar called al-Ālūsī of Baghdad that Allāma Amīnī told his students.

Once, Allāma Amīnī had been confused about a fragment of hadith which he had read in a few books, yet he was keen to verify it in more authoritative Sunni sources. However, any time he asked someone about the source of this narration, he found no convincing reply.

One day in a dream, he saw Imam ʻAlī. The Imam acknowledged that Allāma had been looking for the hadith, and told him that he would find it in a particular book which was in the private library of the home of al-Ālūsī in Baghdad.

Allāma Amīnī started his travel to Baghdad the next day. At that time, it took three days to travel from Najaf to Baghdad. On the first day, he went from Najaf to al-Ḥillah then to Maḥmūdīyah, and on the third day he reached Baghdad. When he reached al-Ālūsī's house, he knocked at the gate and waited. A call came from inside, asking who was knocking. When Allāma replied that it was him, al-Ālūsī quickly opened the door and hugged him, welcoming Allāma Amīnī, him into his house.

As soon as Allāma entered the library, he climbed a ladder to the higher book-shelves, opened the correct book and found the source and hadith he was looking for. When Allāma asked permission to copy the relevant parts of the book, al-Ālūsī was so surprised by what had happened that he asked Allāma how he knew about that particular book, and those hadiths.

Allāma replied that he was looking for some specific information about Imam 'Alī and that he was the one who guided him to this place. Touched by the story, al-Ālūsī began to cry and told Allāma that the whole library now belonged to him, and he could take whatever he liked from it.

Positive Evidence

Al-Ghadīr is not simply a work which seeks to undermine the evidence of those who opposed Imam 'Alī. The positive evidence in support of Imam 'Alī's claim is also assessed. This evidence includes Qur'anic verses which are shown to refer to Imam 'Alī, as well as the hadiths which highlight Imam 'Alī's grandeur and exemplary role and importance. In the sixth volume of *al-Ghadīr*, Allāma Amīnī draws upon Sunni sources to document the birth of Imam 'Alī inside the Ka'bah on the 13 Rajab, thirty years after the Year of the Elephant. After the birth, Imam 'Alī's father, Abū Ṭālib, went inside the Ka'ba and supplicated. His supplication is told by a poet and quoted in *al-Ghadīr*.

O Lord of this worldly darkness and,
O Creator of the bright moon!
May You reveal unto me what name to
choose for this baby.
Thereupon, he heard a herald, addressing him:

O Household of al-Muṣtafā [Prophet Muḥammad]!
You have been particularly distinguished
from the rest of people by means of a pure newborn,
His name has already been determined by the High:
'Alī, derived from the divine attribute al-'Alī
(the Most-High).

Linguisitc Proofs

Once Allāma Amīnī had proved, beyond doubt, that Prophet Muḥammad's sermon at Ghadīr Khumm had certainly taken place, and that the Prophet uttered the words "*man kuntu mawlāhu fahādhā 'Alīyyun mawlāhu*" "For whomever I am a master, this 'Alī is his master", he now turned his attention to ascertaining what the Prophet meant by those words. The need for Allāma's linguistic analysis stems from the way in which the meaning of the texts relating to the Imam 'Alī's right to leadership have been skewed. The degree of distortion has been so great that Allāma Amīnī has spoken of a hegemony of words (*ḥukūmat al-alfāẓ*) which signifies the fact that commonly (unjust) rulers, irrespective of their religions or belief systems, endeavour to commit semantic manipulation of certain keywords disingenuously in order to fool people and achieve their political ends and interests.

Here, Allāma writes about the importance of grammar (in its broad sense) in the Arabic language and argues that to understand the meaning of a word, the grammar of the language must be carefully analysed. Some have argued that "*mawlā*" means "friend" or "a close one"; however, drawing on linguistic analysis, Allāma intended to prove that "*mawlā*" bears a much more significant and binding meaning. He did this through using numerous pieces of Arabic literature, mainly Ghadīr-themed poetry, several hadith discourses from Imams, and Qur'anic verses such as "Your guardian can be only Allah; and His messenger and those who believe, who establish worship and pay the poor due, and bow down [in prayer]." (Sura al-Mā'idah 5:55).

The Role of Poetry

Poetry has always held a special status in Arab and Islamic context and culture. Prophet Muḥammad would encourage poets to compose verses in defence of Islam. Lady Khadījah was also well-known for her poetry which she would use in support of her husband's prophetic mission. One of the main functions of poems was to honour special events. As such, the poems relating to the event of Ghadīr Khumm, which have been handed down through the generations, count as convincing evidence which narrate what happened at the event.[1]

Allāma Amīnī extensively used poems composed by the companions of Prophet Muḥammad to substantiate his case in *al-Ghadīr*. The second volume features ten poems from the first two centuries of Islamic history. Alongside this, poetry from other periods feature in the remaining volumes.

1. It has been said that before *al-Ghadīr* took shape, Allama Amīnī collected a large anthology of Ghadīr-themed Arabic poetry, provisionally entitled "*Shu'arā' al-Ghadīr*" (Poets of al-Ghadīr) and presented it to Grand Ayatollah Sayyid Abū al-Ḥasan Mūsawī Iṣfahānī in Najaf for his advice. Grand Ayatollah Mūsawī Iṣfahānī praised the work yet suggested that only "*al-Ghadīr*" was a sufficient title for the work.

Hisān the Poet

The Iranian poet, late Ḥabīb Chāychīyān who is known as "Ḥisān" (d. 1396 Sh/ 2017) told the present author in a telephone interview that regardless of whether he was in Tehran, Mashad, Karbala, or Najaf, he would always read out his religious poems to Allāma Amīnī so that he could check and correct them. After this, Allāma used to comment on the poems from literary, doctrinal, historical, and conceptual viewpoints. Wherever needed, he would either explain the true historical incident or give him references to relevant books. At times, Allāma Amīnī gave Mr. Chāychīyān some hadiths, historical accounts, or biographies to study so that he could compose religious poems on the themes discussed within them.

The poet emphasized that Allāma Amīnī believed that a truly conscientious and religious poet must be well-versed in the basics of Qur'anic and Islamic articles of faith and Islamic history, all derived from authoritative sources.

Chāychīyān also revealed that he used to attend a series of private lessons in Islamic history and doctrines that Allāma Amīnī offered at his home in Tehran. There were other poets who used to attend the lessons from time to time. He studied *Kāmil al-zīārat* of Ibn Qūlawayh with Allāma Amīnī.

Through his interactions with Mr. Chāychīyān, Allāma Amīnī showed his enthusiasm for educating and training those who produce Islamic literature so that their works would be authentic and powerful. Allāma Amīnī later awarded Mr. Chāychīyān the *takhallus* (poetic signature) "Ḥisān" after Ḥassān b. Thābit, the poet of Prophet Muḥammad) because of his incredible work, who composed the first Ghadīr-themed poem in the world, hence the pioneer in this genre.

As mentioned, the earliest Ghadīr-themed poem was composed by Ḥassān b. Thābit[1] who was present at Ghadīr Khumm. He composed it immediately at the invitation of the Prophet; another indication that Prophet Muḥammad himself intended to have such a historic event marked as a specially significant and blessed occasion; as a day that deserves to remain always memorable.[2]

Qays b. Sa'd b. 'Ubādah used to be a standard-bearer for the Anṣār in some of the wars that the Prophet was forced to fight.[3] Allāma Amīnī quotes Qays's poem relating to Ghadīr Khumm as follows:

> 'Alī is the Imam of ours and everybody, and certain
> Qur'anic verses were revealed in this regard,

1. (d. 40 AH/ 660)

2. By the same token, the fifth, sixth, seventh, and eighth Infallible Imams encouraged their followers to compose poems in order to both commemorate and eternalize the tragic martyrdom of Imam al-Ḥusayn. Similarly, while not related to any specific events, the pilgrimage prayer texts also help to the eternalize the memory of the Prophet's household.

3. The Anṣār (lit. 'helpers') were the residents of Medina who welcomed the Prophet to their city and aided him in the continuation of his mission.

It is the same day when the Prophet said, "Anybody for whom I am the *mawlā*, 'Alī is also the *mawlā*"; this is a tremendous event.

Ismā'īl b. Muḥammad b. Zayd al-Mufarra' al-Ḥimyarī, better known by the name al-Sayyid al-Ḥimyarī[1] has composed twenty-three poems on Ghadīr Khumm, all of which are listed in the second volume of *al-Ghadīr*. Al-Sayyid al-Ḥimyarī was a staunch Shia poet and it was the sixth infallible, Imam Ja'far al-Ṣādiq,[2] who gave him his honorific name. From his poetry, we can note the following verses:

The Prophet enquired,
"Who is more authoritative to you than you yourselves?"
The crowd unanimously answered:
"You are our *mawlā* and more authoritative than us to ourselves; you give us advice."
Then the Prophet remarked:
"Be informed that after me your *mawlā* is 'Alī,
and he is your guide.
Throughout my life, he remains as my vizier,
and shall be your leader after me.
Amongst you, people, may God befriend whoever loves 'Alī, and on their deathbed may they be delighted.
And, whoever feels animosity against 'Alī, may God be their foe and may they be faced with disgrace at death."

Abū Muḥammad Sufyān b. Muṣ'ab al-'Abdī al-Kūfī[3] composed poems which drew strongly upon the Qur'an and hadiths. His poems were so richly loaded with Islamic didactic points that Imam Ja'far al-Ṣādiq advised people to teach

1. 110 AH/ 728-9 – 173 AH/ 789

2. 83-148 AH/ 702-765

3. d. ca. 178 AH/ 794

them to children. His Ghadīr poem comprises eighty-six couplets, of which the following verses provide a flavour.

The house of [the Prophet] Muḥammad
are all meritorious and deserve attention.
Loving them is religiously mandatory
as indicated in the Holy Qur'an.

Indeed, they are the Straight Path
beyond which there remains the throne.
A truthful lady was created for the Truthful,
both of them are the most purified people.

Volume 3 contains eleven Ghadīr poems composed in the third and fourth centuries AH, including a poem in Arabic by an Armenian Christian nobleman, Buqrāṭ b. Ashwat al-Wāmiq.[1]

Isn't it that by Khumm (the Prophet) Muḥammad
stood up and raised 'Alī:
Whoever I am their *mawlā*, after me,
'Alī son of Fāṭimah [b. Asad] is their leader.

Then he prayed:
"O Allah, may you love whoever loves 'Alī,
and be the foe of his enemies,
however it might displease them."

In addition to Buqrāṭ, there have been a number of other Christians who used poetry to express their love of and devotion to the infallible household of Prophet Muḥammad, including Zaynabā b. Isḥāq al-Ras'anī[2].

1. date of death unknown

2. date of death unknown

Some people enquire why Christians,
and other intellectuals, whether Arab or non-Arab,
love them [i.e. the household of the Prophet],

I replied, "I believe every creature, even animals,
love them."

Another Christian, Abū Ya'qūb al-Naṣrānī[1], composed a poem in which he eulogized the Prophet's household.

Good for the paradise tree
which has no parallel in the universe:
Al-Muṣtafā [Prophet Muḥammad] is its trunk,
Fāṭimah its branch,
With 'Alī, the prince of mankind, its fertilizer,
The two Hāshimids [Imams al-Ḥasan and al-Ḥusayn]
are its fruits,
And the Shias are like the leaves found around its fruits.

The fact that Allāma Amīnī quotes Christian Arab poets is an indication of the reverberations of the event of Ghadīr Khumm in that it influenced not only Muslims but also Christians. Allāma Amīnī's approach to Ghadīr-themed poetry was that non-Muslim poets can also be included in the greater realm of Islamic literature. The criterion was not the poet's religion, rather it was the content of the work that counted.

Volume 4 of *al-Ghadīr* focuses on Ghadīr-themed poems of the 4th-6th / 10th-12th centuries. Amongst the poets quoted and profiled, there are such literary luminaries as Ṣāḥib b. al-'Abbād, Sharīf al-Raḍī, Sayyid al-Murtaḍā, and al-Khaṭīb al-Khwārazmī.

1. date of death unknown

Abū al-Qāsim Ismā'īl b. Abī al-Ḥasan 'Abbād b. al-'Abbās b. 'Abbād b. Aḥmad b. Idrīs al-Ṭāliqānī, better known as "Ṣāḥib b. al-'Abbād"[1] was a renowned Shia vizier in the courts of the Persian Shia Buyid (Arabic, Buwayhid) rulers Mu'iyyid al-Dawlah and his brother Fakhr al-Dawlah. As a distinguished man of letters in memory and as an erudite vizier, Ṣāḥib composed many poems, among which several of them deal with the event of Ghadīr Khumm. What follows is just one example:

She enquired,
"Tell me who the leader of this pure faith is."
I said,
"It is the same one who is the noblest of all prophets."
She asked,
"Tell me who attained vicegerency on the Day of Ghadīr."
I answered,
"It is the same one who is the best vicegerent and legatee in Islam."
She insisted,
"Who is this person? Tell me his name!"
I responded,
"He is the Prince of the Faithful, 'Alī b. Abī Ṭālib."

Allāma Amīnī also included the Ghadīr poem written by Abū Ibn al-Ḥajjāj al-Baghdādī,[2] an excerpt of which follows:

O Owner of the Shining Dome at Najaf!
Whoever paid pilgrimage to you and sought treatment was certainly healed.
May Allah not forgive the hypocrites whose spokesman
Congratulated you but later on broke his covenant.

1. d. 385 AH/ 995, in office from 366 AH/ 976 until his death.

2. d. 391 AH/ 1000

Those who paid you the solemn oath of allegiance noticed
That the Prophet announced thus:
This is your leader after me, so whoever appeals to him
Shall neither fear nor grieve.

Abū Muḥammad al-'Awnī[1] is another inspired poet whose Ghadīr poem is discussed by Allāma Amīnī. In a fragment of his poem he makes it clear that the immediate successor to the Prophet is exclusively Imam 'Alī.

God has enshrouded 'Alī with a dress of magnificence
and wisdom, and
Preserved him from worshipping idols.
Other than him, about whom Aḥmad [i.e., Prophet
Muḥammad] said
On the Day of Ghadīr and other days,
That "This brother of mine, is your leader,
As soon as death has come to me."

The two brothers, al-Sharīf al-Raḍī and Sayyid al-Murtaḍā contributed immensely to the cause of Imam 'Alī and Ghadīr literature. Al-Sharīf al-Raḍī has especially been remembered for his compilation of Imam 'Alī's sermons, letters and maxims, chosen for their literary excellence in a book called, *Nahj al-Balāghah* (Path of Eloquence). Allāma Amīnī records the existence of eighty-five book-length commentaries of *Nahj al-Balāghah* since the time it was first compiled (up to his time). Their contributions have been discussed by Allāma.

In his poem of praise for Imam 'Alī, al-Khaṭīb al-Khwārazmī,[2] the well-known Ḥanafite narrator of hadiths, evokes

1. d. 245 AH/ 859
2. d. 568 AH/ 1172

not only the memory of Ghadīr Khumm but also the pivotal role of Imam 'Alī in the Battle of Khaybar.

Is there any nobleman on the earth the same as Abū Turāb
[Imam 'Alī]?
Once I will have an eye ache, I will seek help from the dust
of Abū Turāb's feet.
The discourse of renunciation [from the hypocrites and
infidels], Ghadīr,
And the flag of [the conqueror of] Khaybar is the final
word.

In a fragment of the poem of Ṭalāyi' b. al-Ruzzīk, commonly known as al-Malik al-Ṣāliḥ,[1] we read praise of Imam 'Alī alongside praise of his kinsfolk.

O Strong rope of religion! [O 'Alī!]
O Profound ocean of wisdom!
O Qiblah of the worshipers of Allah!
And, O Ka'ba of the circumambulators!
You belong to a lineage that has always done good
amongst people.
The lineage in which all repent and worship and
who fast and pray.
They are the safeguarders of the precinct of the right path,
always busy with bowing and prostrating to Allah.
You, the infallible members of the
household of the Prophet,
spend the night saying prayers when people sleep.

Ibn al-'Awdī al-Nīlī[2] uses a number of heavenly symbols in his thought-provoking poem on Ghadīr Khumm, a section of which is shown here:

1. martyred 556 AH/ 1161
2. d. 558 AH/ 1162

I have dedicated my special praise to the Prophet
Muḥammad and his counterpart,
For they are matchless in brilliance.
By the fig and the olive [see Sura al-Ṭīn 95:1], it is meant
the progeny of the Prophet,
As those who realize the truth identify them as
The denotation of the tree of Ṭūbā [in Paradise].

Tomorrow [on the Resurrection Day],
the shade and the pool of Kawthar
are none but the household of the Prophet, for
They are the Preserved Tablet
and the hoisted shelter of the divine mercy.
Had it not had been for the sake of
the progeny of Prophet Muḥammad,
Allah would hardly have created the creatures,
neither Adam nor Eve would have descended
on the earth for human progeny.

On the Day of Ghadīr, the Prophet publicly announced the
caliphate of 'Alī, calling to the people:
"The divine command has just reached me to perfect my
prophetic mission,
Now I am communicating it with you:
'Alī is my vicegerent, hence you must only him,
and beware that
as soon as I leave you, he shall be your Imam."

The fifth volume of *al-Ghadīr* contains twelve Ghadīr-themed poems from the sixth and seventh centuries AH, all from certain outstanding figures who had political as well as literary credit.

This includes the poem of Sayyid Muḥammad al-Aqsāsī[1] who was travelling with the Abbasid ruler al-Mustanṣir to Madā'in in Iraq, where Salmān the Persian is buried. Salmān was a close companion of the Prophet and it is said that Imam 'Alī attended his funeral by travelling from Medina to Madā'in and back within the space of a day. Al-Mustanṣir expressed his doubts about how such a rapid journey could have been possible. Al-Aqsāsī responded by saying the land could be traversed by Imam 'Alī through its folding (*ṭayy al-arḍ*), just as it was rapidly traversed by a *jinn* who retrieved the throne of the Queen of Sheba, as testified in the Qur'an, Sura al-Naml (27:39-40). In his poem, he writes:

You have denied the evening in which the vicegerent of the Prophet traversed the land, just when his presence was needed at Madā'in (Ctesiphon).
'Alī washed the body of Salmān, completed the burial, and returned home before dawn.
You claimed it was a statement made by some heretics;
However, what mistake have the exaggerators made if the news is not a lie.

This being so, you do believe that Āṣif b. Barkhīyā in an instant took the throne of Bilqīs
from Sheba to Jerusalem.
It is strange that you have not been a heretic
in your believing the case of Āṣif b. Barkhīyā,
While you regard it as exaggeration to believe the same in the case of Ḥaydar [Imam 'Alī].

As Aḥmad [Prophet Muḥammad] is the noblest of all the prophets,'Alī is the noblest of all vicegerents, unless you would claim all the reports are entirely false.

1. d. 575 AH/ 1179

The aforementioned poetry is a mere fraction of all the poems mentioned in *al-Ghadīr*. By quoting poetry from a diverse range of sources and across several centuries, Allāma Amīnī was able to chart the changes in historical attitudes towards the appointment of Imam 'Alī at Ghadīr Khumm. The poetry, therefore, provides a significant insight into the thoughts of both the scholars and the general public throughout the centuries.

Answering the Critics

Al-Ghadīr has not been discredited since its first volumes were published half a century ago, largely because Allāma Amīnī tried to present his arguments in a way that was irrefutable. For this purpose, he employed various techniques. Firstly, where a hadith was invoked, Allāma Amīnī provided proof of the authenticity of the hadith by listing the full chain of narrators. He also had every hadith he used approved by a number of Sunni scholars, because, as he explained elsewhere, he foresaw the likelihood of people rejecting passages of his text on account of the chain of narration or the hadith itself not being authentic. For the same reason, the second method he used to make *al-Ghadīr* reliable was to quote hadiths, from various chains of hadith relators, so that no doubt remained regarding their authenticity. Thirdly, he provided multiple pieces of evidence, each from different standpoints to give further weight to his arguments.

The Role of Critique

Critiquing counter arguments played an important role and status within *al-Ghadīr*. It is important to note that such critiques were not made out of hostility; instead they were posed sincerely and peacefully, with the aim of uniting different groups of Muslims. From the perspective of Allāma Amīnī, the critiques can be divided into several categories. Firstly, he attempted to tackle those who posed a negative, destructive, and disuniting appraisal of Shiism. For example, at the end of volume 3, Allāma criticised some books of older writers such as *'Iqd al-farīd* of Ibn 'Abd Rabbih, *al-Intiṣār* of Abū al-Ḥusayn Khayyāt, *al-Farq bayn al-firaq* of Abū Manṣūr al-Baghdādī, *al-Fiṣal* of Ibn Ḥazm al-Andulusī, *al-Milal wa al-niḥal* of Muḥammad b. 'Abd al-Karīm al-Shahristānī, *Minhāj al-sunnah* of Ibn Taymīyyah, and *al-Bidāyah wa al-nihāyah* of Ibn Kuthayr as well as several books from modern writers, such as *Muḥāḍarāt ta'rīkh al-umam al-Islāmīyyah* of Sheikh Muḥammad al-Khiḍrī, *Fajr al-Islām* of Aḥmad Amīn, *Jawlah fī rubū' al-sharq al-adnā* of Muḥammad Thābit al-Miṣrī, *al-Ṣurā' bayn al-Islām wa al-wathanīyah* of al-Quṣaymī, and *al-Washī'ah fī naqd 'aqā'id al-Shī'ah* of Mūsā Jār Allāh.

In answering the accusations brought against the Shia sect, Allāma indicated thus:

> Our aim in criticizing these books is to warn the Muslim community and to awaken them to consider the great dangers that these books create for them. This is because they constitute a primary factor in endangering Islamic unity, and dispersing the rank of Muslims.

In volume 3, p. 268, he quotes verbatim Sayyid Rashīd Riḍā's accusation against the Shia sect where he accuses Shias of being pleased at any defeat that other Muslims suffer, so much so that in Iran they celebrated the victory of Russia against the Muslims. In response, Allāma Amīnī said that such lies were forged and fabricated by people like Sayyid Muḥammad Rashīd Riḍā. The Shias of Iran and Iraq are apparently accused by certain Orientalists, explorers, and foreign diplomatic missions and delegations in Muslim countries who have frequented Iran and Iraq and know nothing at all of this happening.

Allāma goes on to argue that the Shias without exception, have respect for the population, blood, honour, and property of all Muslims, both Shias and Sunnis. Therefore, whenever and wherever a calamity befalls the Muslim world, irrespective of the sect it concerns, they have shared its sorrow. The Shias have never limited Islamic brotherhood (the fraternity which has been affirmed by the Qur'an and traditions) only to the Shia world, and have not believed in a difference between the Shias and Sunnis.

One of Allāma Amīnī's important accomplishments in the third volume of *al-Ghadīr* was to refute unfounded and baseless accusations against the followers of Imam 'Alī and to have provided positive evidence in support of the Imam. Some examples of the accusations that Allāma tackled include Ibn 'Abd Rabbih's claims in *al-'Iqd al-farīd* who said that the Shias were like Jews and heathens, and that they have changed the text of the Qur'an. In *al-Fiṣal fī al-milal wa al-ahwā' wa al-nihal*, Ibn Ḥazm al-Andalusī[1] considers Shias to be non-Muslims, accusing them of replacing Qur'anic verses with non-Qur'anic statements. Ibn Ḥazm accuses Shias of believing in the idea that Allah is a created entity, and in the permissibility of a man simultaneously having nine wives in permanent marriage. In *al-Milal wa al-niḥal*, Muḥammad b. 'Abd al-Karīm al-Shahristānī[2] claims that the early Shia theologian, Hishām b. al-Ḥakam, regarded Imam 'Alī as Divine and worthy of worship. He also says the Shia hadith relator, Yūnus b. 'Abd al-Raḥmān al-Qummī, claimed that angels physically carried the Divine throne, and with it

1. d. 456 AH/ 1064
2. d. 548 AH/ 1153

Allah Who was seated therein. In addition to these claims, al-Shahristānī also talks of a Shia sect, the Hishāmīyyah, who in fact never existed. In *al-Intiṣār*, Abū al-Ḥasan al-Khayyāṭ al-Mu'tazilī accuses the Shias of anthropomorphism, or more specifically, the idea that Allah has a physical manifestation which vanish in one place and reappear elsewhere in another form.

Allāma Amīnī also highlighted a consistent attempt throughout Islamic history to deny the merits of Imam 'Alī. For example, the identity of the first Muslim after the Prophet is often disputed. Ibn Kathīr confirms in his history, *al-Bidāyah wa al-nihāyah*, that it was indeed Imam 'Alī who was the first male to accept Islam after the Prophet. However, he undermines this confirmation by stating that the hadiths in support of his view are unreliable. Ibn Kuthayr's position is confusing and it is in fact the case that there are numerous reports from the Prophet which state that Imam 'Alī was the first Muslim. Imam 'Alī's being the first Muslim was also asserted by several companions of the Prophet, including Zayd b. Araqam, Buraydah, 'Abd Allāh b. 'Abbās, 'Umar b. al-Khaṭṭāb, and the aforementioned Anas b. Mālik.

Allāma Amīnī also examined and analysed 200 false ascriptions to Imam 'Alī and distortions in Volume 6 of *al-Ghadīr*.

In the third volume, Allāma Amīnī deals with criticism of incorrect theories. He even devotes extensive time and space to setting out the theories and ideas of Ibn Taymīyyah before carefully criticizing them. He said:

> Ibn Taymīyyah was among those who levelled false accusations against the Ahl al-Bayt and their followers. The

> most important work of Ibn Taymīyyah, *Minhāj al-sunnah*, makes impolite and irrational statements about Shias. One of the characteristics of Ibn Taymīyyah was to defame the Ahl al-Bayt, especially Imam ʻAlī, with hostility and hatred. Despite Qur'anic verses and hadiths supporting the high rank of the Ahl al-Bayt and their virtues (for example in Surahs Āl-i 'Imrān and al-Aḥzāb), and also many Qur'anic verses and hadiths that indicate the orders Prophet Muḥammad issued with regard to respecting his progeny. Ibn Taymīyyah considered respect for the Ahl al-Bayt to be rooted in ignorant thought according to which the head of a tribe was superior to others. Elsewhere, he ascribed such thoughts to Judaism, saying, "Shias believe that only the descendants of ʻAlī deserve to hold Imamate. Judaism also believes that only the family of David deserves to hold government"

Allāma Amīnī noted that Ibn Taymiyyah had never criticized the dynasties of Abū Sufiyān and Marwān, who were hereditary caliphates, and considered them as legitimate Muslim caliphs. However, when it came to the inherited chain of authority in the progeny of Prophet Muḥammad, he attributed hereditary caliphate to ignorant thought, and therefore considered the Imams as not being entitled to caliphate. According to Allāma, one of the biggest faults of Ibn Taymīyyah was his bizarre view of Imam ʻAlī. He denied his virtues and the multitude of Qur'anic verses and hadiths that assert his sublime status and ranking (Tirmadhī; al-Baghawī).

The views of the Orientalist Dwight Martin Donaldson[1] also received critical appraisal in the third volume of *al-Ghadīr*. Donaldson was an American Presbyterian missionary who spent several years in India and Iran. He used to reside in the Iranian shrine city of Mashhad during 1914–40

1. 1884-1976

where he attempted to acquire knowledge of Islam from the religious scholars of the city. During this period, he authored *The Shi'ite Religion* (London, 1933) in which he included some translated passages of Allāma Muḥammad-Bāqir al-Majlisī's *Tuḥfat al-zā'ir*, which is a handbook of pilgrimage rites. After reading an Arabic translation of Donaldson's work (published in Cairo in 1365 AH/ 1964 with the translator's initials 'A. M.'), Allāma Amīnī addressed some misconceptions that Donaldson stated about Islam. For example, Donaldson maintains that Ismā'īl, the eldest son of the sixth Infallible Imam Ja'far al-Ṣādiq, had been nominated to succeed his father; however, since he was "addicted to drunkenness, Musa [*sic*], who was the fourth of the seven sons, had been designated as the next Imam" (Donaldson, *The Shi'ite Religion,* p. 153). Clearly, this is an open affront, a rumour that no Shia accepts.

The third form of critique found in *al-Ghadīr* was Allāma Amīnī's attempt to expose fabricated hadiths about the personalities of Abū Bakr, 'Umar, 'Uthmān, and Mu'āwīyah. The fabricated and forged hadiths are all ascribed to Prophet Muḥammad. Clearly the Prophet never praised any tyrant ruler. It is clear that such fabricated hadiths meant to deceive the Muslim community. In this way, the eighth volume of *al-Ghadīr* examines forty-two virtues fabricated in favor of Abū Bakr, and eleven in respect of 'Umar, and the governance of 'Uthmān. These details include 'Uthmān's unjustified pardoning of 'Umar's son, 'Ubayd Allāh, for the murder of an Iranian Muslim named Hurmuzān and his child. Instead of punishing 'Ubayd Allāh for this crime, 'Uthmān ascended the pulpit and announced that it had been Hurmuzān's fate, and he had forgiven 'Ubayd Allāh. In addition, there are several other accounts of his nepotism. Volume 9 of *al-Ghadīr* continues in this way, surveying the life of 'Uthmān and his wrongdoings based entirely on authentic Sunni accounts and records.

Amīnī turns his attention in the tenth volume of *al-Ghadīr* to documenting the tyranny of the Umayyad dynasty through the use of Sunni sources. This included examining Mu'āwīyah's institution of cursing Imam 'Alī during the call to prayer and after having performed various rituals, as well as the battle against Imam 'Alī in Ṣiffīn, and many others of his tyrant deeds. Volume 11[1] continues to document the crimes of Mu'āwīyah. It includes details of the arbitration trick played on Abū Mūsā al-Ash'arī, and during which Mu'āwīyah made a resolute effort to assert and confirm his political authority.

1. The rest of nine volumes have since remained in manuscript for so far unknown reasons.

After al-Ghadīr

The publication of *al-Ghadīr* followed other outstanding works of Shia scholarship on early Islamic history. These include: *Abaqāt al-anwār* by Allāma Mir Ḥāmid Ḥusayn Mūsawī Nayshābūrī[1] of Lucknow, India, and *al-Murāji'āt* by the Lebanese Shia scholar Sayyid Sharaf al-Dīn al-'Āmilī.[2] But *al-Ghadīr* was unique in its rigour. Assessing and drawing on early first-hand accounts, reports, hadiths, and poetry in order to shed light on every detail relevant to the event of Ghadīr Khumm, Allāma Amīnī studied over 10,000 books from cover to cover, and checked and cited over 100,000. The result of Allāma Amīnī's endeavours was an organized collection of quotations and arguments from important and reliable Sunni resources, including works of history, poetical anthologies, hadith collections, and Qur'anic commentaries.

Al-Ghadīr was published twice in Allāma Amīnī's lifetime. The first publication was the Najaf edition, published in nine volumes in 1364-71 AH/ 1945-52. The next publication was the revised edition, published in eleven volumes in Tehran in 1372 AH/ 1953. The revised edition has subsequently been reprinted many times in Beirut, Tehran, and Qum, and has also been abridged many times in Persian and Arabic.[3] Some of the volumes of *al-Ghadīr* were translated

1. d. 1306 AH/ 1888

2. d. 1290-1377 AH/ 1872-1957

3. Of all the abridged editions and introductions available in Persian, *Siyrī dar al-Ghadīr* (Qum, 1370 Sh/ 1989) is the most concise and the most faithful. Comprising 173 pages, the abridgment was a joint endeavor of two of Allama Amīnī's sons, Sheikh Aḥmad and Dr. Muḥammad Amīnī-Najafī.

into Persian by the Tehran-based *mujtahid* Ayatollah Sayyid Muḥammad-Taqī Wāḥidī[1] under the direct supervision of the late Allāma Amīnī.[2] Muḥammad-Riḍā Ḥakīmī also played a key role in introducing Allāma Amīnī's *al-Ghadīr* to Iran and making its significance known. He even used *al-Ghadīr* in his own works to illustrate that the successorship of Imam 'Alī can be seen as concordant with the Divine plan to guide humanity. Perhaps without Ḥakīmī, *al-Ghadīr* would not have received much attention among Persian speakers and particularly in Iran.

Conclusion

With a fair and balanced approach, *al-Ghadīr* allows the conscientious reader to make up his own mind about the successorship of Prophet Muḥammad. Allāma Amīnī presents the relevant and convincing facts and avoids using an antagonistic tone, thereby making it possible for non-Shias, Muslim and non-Muslims alike, to appreciate his work. Amongst the non-Shias who wrote to Allāma Amīnī in praise of *al-Ghadīr* are Boulos Salāmih (the Lebanese Christian literary figure); Sheikh Muḥammad Sa'īd Daḥdūḥ of Aleppo;

1. 1276-1359 Sh/ 1897-1980

2. The Persian translation of *al-Ghadīr* by Ayatollah Wāḥidī is prefaced by a short note written by Allama Amīnī and dated 27 Jamaadi II 1380/ 1960. In the note, Allama Amīnī gives his blessing for Ayatollah Wāḥidī's undertaking provided that he remains faithful to the original. See Allama Amīnī, *al-Ghadīr*, vol. 1, trans. by Sayyid Muḥammad-Taqī Wāḥidī (Tehran, 1381 AH/ 1340 Sh/ 1961), p. 172. An earlier Persian translation of *al-Ghadīr* was undertaken by Sayyid Mujtabā Navvāb-Ṣafavī (executed 1375 AH/ 1334 Sh/ 1955). Sayyid Navvāb-Ṣafavī, who used to be a student of the seminary in Najaf, undertook the translation at the suggestion of Allama Amīnī. However, due to his political activities against the Pahlavis and against the British involvement in Iran he was too occupied to translate more than the first volume. See Muḥammad-Hādī al-Amīnī, *Mu'jam rijāl al-fikr wa al-adab fī al-Najaf khilāl alf 'ām*, 2nd edn., 3 vols. (n.p., 1413 AH/ 1992), pp. 1301-03.

Muḥammad ʻAbd al-Ghanī Ḥasan of Cairo; the Zaidite imam of Yemen, Yaḥyā b. Muḥammad Ḥamīd al-Dīn; ʻAbd Allāh b. al-Ḥusayn of Amman, Jordan; Dr. Muḥammad Ghallāb of Cairo; ʻAbd al-Raḥmān al-Kīyālī of Cairo; the Iraqi lawyer, Dr. Tawfīq al-Fukaykī of Baghdad; the British-Iraqi Arabist, Dr. Safa Khulusi; Sheikh Muḥammad Saʻīd al-ʻUrfī of Damascus; the renowned Lebanese scholar, Ayatollah Sayyid ʻAbd al-Ḥusayn Sharaf al-Dīn; Grand Ayatollah Sayyid Muḥsin al-Ḥakīm of Najaf; the former Iraqi prime minister, Sayyid Muḥammad al-Ṣadr; Asʻad Dāghir of Beirut; Sayyid Mahdī al-Muntafikī of Baghdad; Dr. Muṣṭafā Jawād of Baghdad; and Sheikh Muḥammad Taysīr al-Shāmī of Damascus. Many of these letters are included in editions of *al-Ghadīr*. All together, the letters alone would make a substantial volume.

Al-Ghadīr answers the major objections concerning the leadership of Imam ʻAlī. It provides for a better understanding and appreciation of the Ghadīr Khumm sermon and its context. As a defender of the Prophet's household, Allāma Amīnī will be remembered along with such important Shia scholars such as Sheikh al-Mufīd.[1]

1. For an account of Sheikh al-Mufid and his doctrinal contribution, see M. McDermott, *The Theology of al-Shaikh al-Mufīd* (1978); and Bayhom-Daou, *Sheikh Mufīd* (2005). d. 413 AD/ 1022.

PART THREE

THE QUEST FOR KNOWLEDGE

"The scholar is the one who is never satiated with knowledge and never becomes full of it"

- IMAM 'ALĪ

Allāma Amīnī's Travels

Allāma Amīnī's research for *al-Ghadīr* inevitably meant that he spent a considerable amount of his life in both public and private libraries. It has been mentioned that Allāma Amīnī would become so engrossed in the manuscripts and other texts he pored over that he would be entirely heedless of distractions. He would copy manuscripts, take notes from any work that had relevance to his project, and weep whenever he discovered the instances of tyranny and injustice perpetrated against the Prophet's household.

Iraq

Allāma Amīnī spent much of his time in the rich traditional archives of books affiliated to the shrine of Imam 'Alī in Najaf, Iraq. Founded by the Najaf-based, Iranian scholar Sheikh Hajj Muḥammad-'Alī Najaf-Ābādī in 1332 AH/ 1913, this library was the first traditional book archive in Najaf. It consisted of a large room that housed around 10,000 books amongst which there were 4,000 precious manuscripts. Instead of a team of well-trained, specialist staff, the library used to be managed by a single caretaker who would open and close its gate without any other service to those who used to go there.

In addition to the aforementioned book archive, Allāma Amīnī visited and benefited from the private libraries of several outstanding Shia clerics of Najaf. They were as follows: Ayatollah Sayyid Ja'far Baḥr al-'Ulūm,[1] Ayatollah Sayyid Muḥammad Baḥr al-'Ulūm whose founder was

1. d. 1957

Sayyid Muḥammad-Ṣādiq Baḥr al-'Ulūm,[1] Ayatollah Sheikh Muḥammad-Ḥusayn Kāshif al-Ghiṭā',[2] Ayatollah Sheikh Muḥammad Ṭāhir al-Samāwī,[3] and Ayatollah Muḥammad-Riḍā Faraj-Allāh al-Najafī.[4] Allāma Amīnī visited the library affiliated to the Najaf-based *ḥusaynīyyah* of the inhabitants of Shushtar, a city in the southwest of Iran.

Within Karbala there are many fine libraries established by senior Shia clerics of the city. Allāma Amīnī visited the private libraries of the late Ayatollah Sheikh 'Abd al-Ḥusayn Tihrānī and Sheikh Muḥsin Abū al-Ḥabb al-Ḥā'irī.

He also visited the libraries of Baghdad and neighbouring al-Kāẓimīyyah. These include the public library of the Āl al-Ḥaydarī *ḥusayniyyah,*[5] as well as the private libraries of Ayatollah Sayyid Ḥasan al-Ṣadr al-Kāẓimī, Sheikh Mahdī b. Ḥasan Kubbah, Sayyid 'Īsā al-'Aṭṭār, and Sheikh Muḥammad-Riḍā Shāljī (Shalchī) Mūsā al-Kāẓimī. Allāma Amīnī also visited the libraries of Basra, al-Hilla, and of the shrine city Samarra, where the library of Ayatollah Sheikh Muḥammad 'Askarī-Tihrānī is located.

1. d. 1897

2. d. 1952

3. d. 1951

4. d. 1967

5. A *ḥusayniyyah* is an assembly hall, usually used to commemorate the martyrdom of Imam al-Ḥusayn in the months Muharram and Safar. In southern India, a *ḥusayniyyah* is called an *Ashura Khana* (derived from the Persian phrase *'Āshūr Khāneh*) and in northern India it is called an *imambara*. See G. Thaiss, "Ḥusaynīyah" in *The Oxford Encyclopedia of the Modern Islamic World*, ed. J. L. Esposito (4 vols.; New York, 1995), vol. 2, pp. 153-155. For the Indian context, see Sayyid Sadiq Naqvi, *The Ashūr Khānas of Hyderabad City* (3rd ed., Hyderabad, 2006).

Iran

In Iran, Allāma Amīnī made use of the major libraries. They include The National Parliamentary Library in Tehran, the Āstān-i Quds-i Raḍawī Library in Mashhad, and some important libraries in Qum, Kermanshah, and Hamadan.

India

Despite Turkey and other Arab countries being near Iraq, Allāma Amīnī headed to India to conduct his research. This was because the Indian subcontinent has long been famous as a pluralistic and multi-religious nation. Peaceful co-existence of the followers of Islam, Hinduism, and other religions for several centuries, and the respect Hindus received from various Shia dynasties in India made it a fitting ground for Muslims to preserve copies of their major religious and academic legacies there. In addition, there have been many Indian Shia students and scholars in Najaf that could have influenced Allāma Amīnī's decision to go there for research purposes. Accompanied by two research assistants namely his son, Hajj Sheikh Riḍā and his brother-in-law, Sayyid Ghulām-Riḍā Kasā'ī, Allāma Amīnī took a five-hour flight from Baghdad to Mumbai. At the Mumbai airport, Allāma Amīnī received a warm welcome from a number of Muslim dignitaries including Raja Kumar Amir Muḥammad Ḥyder Khan. They were taken to the Sea Face Hotel, built by the Muslim charity founded by Hajj Muḥammad 'Alī Ḥabīb. Amongst the Mumbai residents who visited Allāma Amīnī during the eight days they spent at the hotel were Hajj Sheikh Muḥammad Ḥasan Najafī, Maharaja Amir Ḥyder Khan, Sayyid 'Abbās Rizvi Hyderabadi, and Sheikh Muḥammad Ḥasan 'Irfānī and his sons.

During his stay, Allāma Amīnī took the opportunity to

visit the Asiatic Society of Bombay. Founded in 1804 by Sir James Mackintosh, it possesses a library with a valuable collection of books and manuscripts written in Arabic, Persian, Urdu, English, French, German, and Sanskrit. The curator of the library presented two series of its journals to Allāma Amīnī in appreciation.

Then, in the beginning of Ramadan 1380 AH/ 1960, Allāma and his colleagues travelled by train to Lucknow, in northern India, accompanied by Muḥammad Hyder Khan. They were warmly welcomed by Sayyid Muḥammad Sa'īd Allāh and his brother Sayyid Nāṣir al-Millah, grandsons of Mir Ḥāmid Ḥusayn. In Lucknow, Allāma Amīnī visited the Nāṣirīyah Library founded by the Iranian *mujtahid* Sayyid Muḥammad Qulī Mūsawī Nayshābūrī.[1] His library was enriched by his son, Mir Ḥāmid Ḥusayn[2], and his grandson Sayyid Nāṣir Ḥusayn, who both donated their private collections. At the time Allāma Amīnī visited it, the Nāṣiriyyah Library (perhaps named after its curator rather than its founder) contained over 30,000 printed books and manuscripts in Urdu, Persian, and Arabic.

Allāma Amīnī found a number of precious manuscripts in the Nāṣiriyyah Library which greatly helped his *al-Ghadīr* project. Some of the texts that Allāma Amīnī transcribed or made notes on were as follows: the *Manāqib* of the Shāfi'ite jurist Ibn al-Maghāzilī,[3] which was transcribed from a 585 AH/ 1189 version in 300 folios; *Miftāḥ al-najā fī manāqib āl al-'abā* of Mirza Muḥammad b. Rustam al-Ḥārithī al-Badakhshī, written in 1123 AH/1711 in 320 folios and the 494 folios of *Alal-Ṣirāṭ al-sawīyy fī manāqib āl al-Nabīyy* by Sayyid

1. d. 1260 AH/ 1844
2. d. 1306 AH/ 1888
3. d. 483 AH/ 1090

Maḥmūd al-Shīkhānī al-Qādirī al-Madanī. Of the 494 folios, Allāma Amīnī himself transcribed around 400 folios. The rest was completed by his research assistants.

He also made use of the libraries in the religious colleges (*madrasahs*) he visited in Lucknow. The Madrasat al-Wa'izin, so named for its training of Muslim preachers, was originally established in 1338 AH/ 1919 by Ayatollah Sayyid Najm Ḥasan. The *madrasah* taught English to its students and published periodicals in English as well as in Urdu, respectively entitled *The Muslim Review* and *al-Wa'iz.* The library contained over 20,000 books and manuscripts in Urdu, Persian, Arabic, and English.

Although first established in Kanpur in 1894, the Dār al-'Ulūm Nudwat al-'Ulamā was later moved to Lucknow. When Allāma Amīnī visited its library, it held around 60,000 books, some of which he would find very helpful for his project. Important sources discovered here include *Al-Ṣawā'iq al-mursalah 'alā al-jahamīyyah wa al-mu'aṭṭalah* of Shams al-Dīn Abī 'Abd Allāh Muḥammad b. Qayyim al-Jawzīyy;[1] *al-Mu'jam al-ṣaghīr* of Hafiz Abū al-Qāsim Sulaymān al-Ṭabarānī[2]; and the *Musnad* of Hafiz 'Abd b. Ḥamīd Abī Muḥammad al-Kashshī[3]. Today, the library has an impressive 150,000 books, of which around 5,500 are precious volumes in Arabic, Persian, and Urdu.

The Mumtāz al-'Ulamā Library was named after the unofficial title of its founder, the celebrated local Shia *mujtahid* Sayyid Muḥammad Taqī b. Sayyid Ḥusayn b. Sayyid Dildār 'Alī[4]. Sayyid Muḥammad Taqī had written at least ten books

1. d. 751 AH/ 1350
2. d. 360 AH/ 970
3. d. 249 AH/ 863
4. d. 249 AH/ 863

on doctrinal and religious topics, and his library contained 18,000 books and manuscripts in Arabic, Persian, and Urdu. In addition to finding a manuscript of *Al-Kashf wa al-bayān fī tafsīr al-Qur'ān* by Abū Is'ḥāq Aḥmad b. Muḥammad al-Tha'labī here, in the same library, Allāma Amīnī also discovered an old and precious codex of *Ṣaḥīfah al-Sajjādīyyah*; the well-known collection of supplications taught by the fourth Imam 'Alī b. al-Ḥusayn, known as "al-Sajjād". The codex was in the hand of 'Alī b. Sukūn and annotated by a number of scholars. The first annotation was written by Shia scholar Shams al-Dīn Muḥammad b. Makkī b. Muḥammad – the 'First Martyr'.[1]

In the Firangi Mahal Library Allāma Amīnī found many more precious books and manuscripts. Among them, he had access to a manuscript of *Mashāriq al-ishrāq ilā maṣāri' al-'ushshāq* by Ibn Nuḥās Aḥmad b. Ibrāhīm al-Dimashqī which was apparently copied in 1122 AH/ 1710. The Firangi Mahal Library was founded in 1230 AH/ 1814 by Qīyām al-Dīn 'Abd al-Qādir of Lucknow and is home to over 4,000 books in Arabic, Persian, and Urdu. Its name is derived from the Persian word for 'foreign' due to the fact that its building once belonged to French traders four centuries ago.

The last of the Lucknow libraries was the Amīr al-Dawlah Public Library. Established in 1868 by the British Indian Association of Oudh in memory of the late Amīr al-Dawlah, its building was erected by Amir Muḥammad Ḥasan Khan Raja Maḥmūd Ābād, who donated to it 55,000 books from his own private library. At the time Allāma Amīnī visited it, the library housed over 110,000 volumes in Arabic, Persian, Urdu, English, and Sanskrit. Amongst the Sanskrit manuscripts in the library, there were sacred Hindu texts dating back to 4,000 years ago.

1. martyred 786 AH/ 1384

During his stay in Lucknow, Allāma Amīnī received several invitations from the Muslim community of Kanpur. While he could spend only two days in the city, Allāma accepted the invitations on the basis that the visit could benefit his research. He travelled by train with his research assistants and Professor Sayyid Yāwar Mahdī. Since his trip coincided with the anniversary of Imam 'Alī's martyrdom on the 21st Ramadan, Allāma Amīnī delivered lectures to commemorate the occasion. According to some accounts, crowds of over 10,000 gathered to listen to Allāma Amīnī, who spoke in Persian while an interpreter translated into Urdu.

Allāma Amīnī delivering lectures in Lucknow

In Kanpur, Allāma Amīnī was invited to Aligarh University by Professor Dr. Sayyid Sibṭ al-Ḥasan Fāḍil Ḥasnawī (director of the Islamic collection at Aligarh Muslim Public Library), and welcomed by the rector, Dr. Bashīr Ḥusayn Zayidī.

Originally known as the Mohammadan Anglo-Oriental College, Aligarh Muslim University was established in 1875 by Sir Sayyid Aḥmad Khan (1817–1898) and its name was changed in 1920.

The central library of Aligarh Muslim University proudly housed over 500,000 volumes, a collection which would later grow to 1,400,000. The Oriental division had 200,000 books, with 10,000 of them in Arabic, Persian, and Urdu, with the rest of books in English as well as in other local languages. Amongst the precious rare books was a copy of a work printed and published in Rome in 1593 by the great Iranian Muslim sage, philosopher, and physician, Avicenna known in Arabic and Persian as Ibn Sīnā[1].

The manuscripts and rare books that Allāma Amīnī discovered here included an early manuscript of the *Nahj al-Balāghah* dated 533 AH/ 1138; a copy of *Ṣiḥāḥ al-lughāh* by Abū Naṣr Ismā'īl al-Jawharī[2] that was transcribed in 648 AH/ 1250; *Talkhīṣ al-muwāfiqah* by Jār Allāh al-Zamakhsharī;[3] an abridged 100 folio version of *al-Muwāfaqah* of Ḥafiz Ibn Sammān al-Rāzī[4] ; and *al-Maṣnū ' fī ḥadīth al-mawḍū'* by Nūr al-Dīn 'Alī b. Sulṭān Muḥammad al-Hirawī, also known as Mulla 'Alī Qārī.[5]

1. d. 427 AH/ 1035
2. d. 393 AH/ 1002
3. d. 538 AH/ 1143
4. d. 445 AH/ 1053
5. d. 1014 AH/ 1605

While in Aligarh, the sad news of the death of Grand Ayatollah Sayyid Ḥusayn Burūjirdī,[1] a pillar of the Qum seminary, was announced. As the news spread throughout India, telegrams of condolence were sent to the religious authorities of Najaf and Qum. Allāma Amīnī sought solace in Agra by the tomb of the late Qāḍī Nūr Allāh Shūshtarī, a renowned Iranian Shia scholar and leading *mujtahid* who was martyred in 1019 AH/ 1610. Allāma Amīnī arranged for a ceremony in memory of Ayatollah Burūjirdī along with Sayyid Sibṭ al-Ḥasan, a renowned Shia cleric of Agra.

Although Allāma Amīnī initially declined the invitation to visit Jalali, a small town to the west of Aligarh, due to his research commitments, the insistence of one of its leading Shia figures, Nawab Sayyid ʻAlī Aẓhar, meant that he eventually spent a day there.

Sayyid Sibṭ al-Ḥasan accompanied Allāma Amīnī and his companions on the trip from Aligarh to Jalali. At the Jalali Central Mosque, built in 665 AH/ 1266, Allāma Amīnī led the five daily prayers. After the evening prayer, Sayyid Sibṭ al-Ḥasan addressed the congregation to introduce Allāma Amīnī and his great research project.

Having stayed in Aligarh for 24 days, Allāma Amīnī and his research assistants continued on to Rampur, in the state of Uttar Pradesh, where they were welcomed by the Maharaja of Rampur, Amir ʻAlīraza Khan. Allāma Amīnī was hosted in the palace of Sayyid Muḥammad Ḥāmid ʻAlī Khan and was provided with the necessary facilities for the continuation of his research, including access to the Raza Library. Established by Nawab Fayḍ Allāh Khan, who ruled Rampur from 1774–1794, the Raza Library is still an important repository of the Islamic cultural heritage of northern

1. 1292-1380 AH/ 1875-1960

India, containing at least 30,000 printed books and periodicals.

In the Raza Library, Allāma discovered the *Ma'ānī al-akhbār* (commonly known as *Baḥr al-fawā'id*), of Abū Bakr 'Umar b. Abī Is'ḥāq Ibrāhīm al-Kilābādhī al-Bukhārī[1] who also wrote the book *al-Ta'arruf fī al-taṣawwuf*. Other books that Allāma discovered there included: *al-Nukat wa al-'uyūn fī tafsīr al-Qur'ān al-Karīm* of Abī al-Ḥasan 'Alī b. Muḥammad b. Ḥabīb al-Baṣrī al-Shāfi'ī[2] who is the author of *al-Aḥkām al-sulṭānīyyah*. Other works uncovered by Allāma Amīnī in the Raza Library include *al-Fuṣūl al-sittah* of Muḥammad b. Muḥammad al-Bukhārī, commonly known as Khwājah Pārsā[3] and *al-Khayr al-jārī fī sharḥ Ṣaḥīḥ al-Bukhārī* of Mulla Ya'qūb al-Banbānī.[4]

Hyderabad, with its rich historical archives, could have hardly been overlooked by Allāma Amīnī during his Indian excursion. One of the Hyderabad libraries that he visited was the Salar Jung Museum and Library which had been established by Mir Yūsuf 'Alī Khan, Salar Jung III (1889–1949), the prime minister of the seventh Nizam (monarch) of Hyderabad. Its precious manuscripts amount to 8,000 volumes, of which 2,500 items were in Arabic, Persian, and Urdu, with the rest in other Indian languages as well as in English. Altogether, the library's holdings amount to over 60,000 titles, of which around 50,000 titles are in Asian and Islamicate languages. Another place Allāma also visited was the library of Osmania University. Established in 1918, its library housed over 500,000 books in the time of Allāma,

1. d. 384 AH/ 994
2. d. 450 AH/ 1058
3. d. 822 AH/ 1419
4. d. 1098 AH/ 1686

with over 6,000 manuscripts in Urdu, Arabic, Persian, and other languages. The third library Allāma Amīnī visited in Hyderabad was the State Central Library, commonly known as the Aṣifīyah Library and established in 1819 by Nawab Sayyid Ḥusayn Bilgrami,[1] commonly known as 'Imād al-Mulk Bahādur.

Allāma Amīnī's research trip to India gave rise to many scholarly exchanges and discoveries. The final visit of his stay was to the Khoda Bakhsh Oriental Library in Patna, in the state of Bihar. Established in 1819 by Khan Bahādur Khudā Bakhsh,[2] this library housed around 21,000 Oriental manuscripts.

Syria

In the summer of 1384 AH/1965 at the suggestion of the late Ayatollah Sayyid 'Abd al-'Azīz Ṭabāṭabā'ī Yazdī, Allāma Amīnī travelled to Syria and stayed there for four months. He spent the majority of his time in Damascus, and visited the library of the Madrasat al-Ẓahirīyyah, where he took notes from around 590 manuscripts. Madrasah al-Ẓāhirīyyah was founded in the al-'Imārah district in 678 AH/ 1276 by Sa'īd b. al-Ẓāhir. The library achieved national recognition by 1880, thanks to its 100,000 printed books and 13,000 manuscripts.

Allāma Amīnī also visited the library of the Arab Academy during his stay. Founded in 1919, it had long been a notable research organization which had attracted prominent Arabists and Orientalists such as Muḥammad Kurd

1. 1842-1926
2. 1842–1908

'Alī,[1] Fares al-Khouri,[2] Taha Hussein,[3] Philip K. Hitti,[4] Ernest Herzfeld,[5] Carl Brockelmann,[6] Louis Massignon,[7] Sir H. A. R. Gibb,[8] and I. Kratchekovski[9] among many others.

In Rabi' al-Awwal 1384 AH/ September 1964, Allāma Amīnī travelled to the Allepo branch of the Syrian National Library, established in 1924 and home to 100,000 books in Damascus. This city was once the capital of the Shia Ḥamdānid dynasty (890–1004) in the Levant.

Altogether, Allāma Amīnī stayed in Aleppo for 22 days and visited a number of libraries, including Madrasat al-Aḥmadīyyah, established in 1724. He consulted thirteen important manuscripts in the city and had a number of important discussions with learned dignitaries such as Sheikh Muḥammad Sa'īd Daḥdūḥ and Sheikh 'Alī Kamāl, the curator of Madrasat al-Aḥmadiyyah. A report of Allāma Amīnī's discussions is available in his *Sīratunā wa sunnatunā sīrah nabīyyinā wa sunnatih* (Najaf, 1384 AH/1965).[10]

Turkey

Allāma Amīnī's last research trip was to Turkey in 1387 AH/ 1967. At this stage of his life, his health was declining due to his struggle with cancer. Yet he stayed in Turkey for

1. d. 1053
2. d. 1962
3. d. 1973
4. d. 1978
5. d. 1948
6. d. 1956
7. d. 1962
8. d. 1971
9. d. 1951
10. I am currently engaged in translating this book into English.

25 days of which he spent 15 days in Istanbul, and 10 days in Bursa.

Istanbul had been the capital of the vast Ottoman Empire (1299-1923), and the city of important libraries and rich archives. According to his son, Ayatollah Sheikh Riḍā Amīnī, Allāma Amīnī visited the 74,000 manuscripts of the Suleymania Library, established in 1927, the Topkapi Palace Museum and Library, established in 1928, with around 13,450 manuscripts, and the main library of the Ayasofya Mosque, and the Nuruosmaniye Mosque Library, built in 1755.

Bursa is found in the Marmara region of Northwest Turkey. Upon his arrival there, Allāma Amīnī headed to the Grand Mosque which was built from 1369 to 1399, and holds a library with valuable manuscripts. The Huseyin Çelebi (pronounced Chelebi) Library, which Allāma Amīnī also visited, has another manuscript collection.

Due to his ill health Allāma Amīnī was unable to work as he did in India and Syria. Despite this difficulty, he still managed to take notes from around fifty-five Arabic and Islamic manuscripts. Realizing that this was by no means enough, he asked his son, Sheikh Riḍā, and Sayyid ʻAbd al-ʻAzīz Ṭabāṭabā'ī Yazdī[1] to initiate a project that would make the extraordinary Turkish collections more accessible to the scholars of Najaf. Accordingly, Sheikh Riḍā and Sayyid ʻAbd al-ʻAzīz captured around 700,000 Turkish works on microfilm. This was finally completed after the death of Allāma Amīnī, and their microfilms currently enriched the Imām Amīr al-Mu'minīn Public Library in Najaf.

1. d. 1416 AH/ 1374 Sh/ 1996

Other Travels

Allāma Amīnī was always on the lookout for new research material; however, there were times when he travelled for purposes other than research.

Allāma Amīnī completed his first Hajj pilgrimage to Mecca and Medina in 1355 AH/ 1936. In 1375 AH/ 1955, he performed the Hajj again.

In 1365 AH/ 1945, he took a trip to Iran, where he visited Kermanshah and Mashhad. It seems that he stayed in Mashhad for the entire month of Ramadan. He delivered lectures and sermons at Mu'tamid Khan Mosque for ten nights.

Then, in Safar 1376 AH/ September 1956, Allāma Amīnī stayed in Isfahan for a month. This was a good opportunity to introduce the people of Isfahan to *al-Ghadīr*; he often requested to lead prayers and deliver sermons. He was invited to towns and villages bordering Isfahan, such as Najafābād, Rīz, and Dastguīr, where he was always welcomed by local scholars and dignitaries. Among the scholars Allāma Amīnī met were Ayatollah Rowḍātī, Ayatollah Khādimī, Ayatollah Sayyid Shaftī. In Najafābād, Allāma Amīnī was welcomed by Ayatollah Ḥusayn-'Alī Muntaẓirī. 6,000 well-wishers came to bid him farewell as he left Isfahan for Najaf via Tehran at the end of Safar.

It appears that Allāma Amīnī had visited London several times. During his first trip in 1383 AH/ 1963, he wrote a letter to the Mashhad-based Grand Ayatollah Sayyid 'Abd al-Hādī Mīlānī.[1] There is no record of Allāma Amīnī having visited the British Library, or any other important research

1. d. 1354 Sh/ 1975

libraries, although it would have been out of character if he did not take the opportunity to do so. His second trip to London took place in 1968 for medical treatment, and his last visit to London was in 1970, about a month before his death.

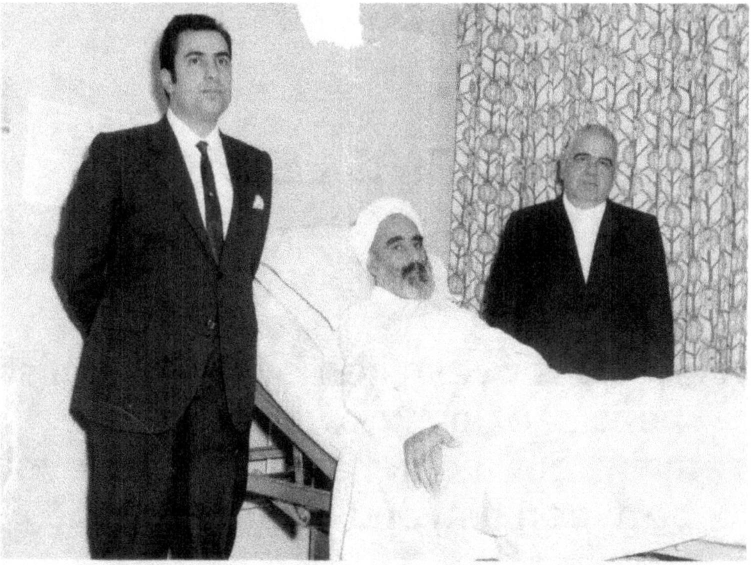

Allāma Amīnī at the Ariya Hospital with Mr. Faraj Allah Mowahhedi, a merchant in Tehran, 1970.

PART FOUR

A LASTING LEGACY

"He who is overtaken by death whilst he is seeking knowledge, there remains but a difference of one level between him and the Prophets."

- IMAM ʿALĪ

The Final Years

Allāma Amīnī battled with spinal cancer for almost seven years. Since he was constantly engrossed in research, he had at times been inattentive to his own health. His illness constrained him, largely keeping him in his home. On occasion, he would seek the medical advice of doctors in Najaf and Baghdad. In the summer when he would stay in Tehran where he could be closer to his family, he would visit some of the rich libraries, and also benefit from more specialist medical advice.

It was Allāma Amīnī's doctors in Tehran who suggested that he travel to London for more advanced medical treatment. At the time of his last month-long trip to London in 1970 with his relatives, his condition had worsened and there was little that could be done to treat him. His return to Tehran saw him bedridden, and often unable to continue his beloved research project for *al-Ghadīr*.

Allāma Amīnī was taken to Ārīyā Hospital in Tehran on 18 Rabi al-Thani 1390 AH/ 23 June 1970. Within a week, on 25 Rabi al-Thani 1390 AH/ 30 June 1970, his condition became critical. Allāma Amīnī's doctors were unable to do anything further to cure his illness, so he was taken back to his home in Shu'ā' al-Dawlah Alley. Three days later, at 11:10 am on Friday 28 Rabi al-Thani 1390 AH/ 3 July 1970, Allāma Amīnī breathed his last.[1]

1. Although the date of death inscribed on Allama Amīnī's tombstone reads 10 Rabi al-Thani 1390/ 14 June 1970, from a study of various documents, including the works of his son, Ayatollah Sheikh Riḍā Amīnī, it is clear that this is not the correct date.

Mourning Imam Husayn

During the last days of his life in Tehran, Allāma Amīnī told his son, Ayatollah Sheikh Riḍā Amīnī, that upon recovering from his illness, he would like to move to Karbala so that he could mourn Imam al-Ḥusayn's tragic martyrdom for at least five years.

At the time of his death, Allāma Amīnī was 68 years of age. The next morning, his body was washed and carried to the Ark Mosque before going to the mortuary. After another ceremony, his body was taken to Baghdad on a flight which departed from Tehran at 5.00 p.m. An earlier flight could not be taken because the ex-Baathist authorities of Iraq refused to grant permission for Allāma Amīnī's burial in Najaf. Apparently, a number of Arab countries had urged against Allāma Amīnī's burial in Najaf on account of their misconceptions of *al-Ghadīr*.

However, due to the much stronger protests from the Shia authorities of Najaf and Karbala, as well as several other cities, the Iraqi authorities eventually allowed the body of Allāma Amīnī to be flown to Baghdad for burial in Najaf. The sons of Grand Ayatollah Sayyid Muḥsin al-Ḥakīm[1] and Grand Ayatollah Sayyid Abū al-Qāsim Mūsawī Khu'ī[2] had been instrumental in making the burial possible.

1. d. 1390 AH/ 1970
2. d. 1413 AH/ 1992

Organised by the sons of the Ayatollah Sayyid Muḥsin al-Ḥakīm, a large crowd of mourners, including around a hundred Shia clerics, gathered at Baghdad International Airport. Allāma Amīnī's body was taken to the al-Kāẓimīyyah holy shrine where the two seventh and ninth infallible Imams, Mūsā b. Ja'far and Muḥammad al-Taqī are buried and then to Karbala before resting in Najaf. There friends, colleagues and children kept a constant vigil by reciting the Holy Qur'an in the mosque of the Najaf Religious University, in Arabic Jāmi'ah al-Najaf al-Dīnīyyah.

The next day, Sunday 8 Jamadi al-Awwal 1370 AH/ 12 July 1970, a large funeral procession was held. The funeral prayers, led by Grand Ayatollah Khu'ī, were said over the body of Allāma Amīnī in the courtyard of Imam 'Alī's shrine, after which the body was symbolically taken around the tomb of the Imam. In accordance with the preparations he had already made for the location of his burial, Allāma's body was finally buried in the basement of the Imam Amīr al-Mu'minīn Public Library which he had founded. Upon his burial, Muḥammad-Riḍā Ḥakīmī remarked that "two libraries now laid side by side".[1]

1. Ḥakīmī, *Ḥimāsih-yi Ghadīr*, p. 345.

Perhaps not realizing the full extent of his scholarly contribution, or perhaps due to a lack of interest in religion and scholarship, the Iranian media of the day (during the ex-Pahlavi royal dynasty) gave little coverage to the death of Allāma Amīnī. Yet news of his death reverberated throughout Iran, Iraq, and other Muslim lands and numerous memorial services were held.

Allāma Amīnī's first wife returned to Iran the year following his death. She passed away in 1356 Sh/ 1977 and was buried in the Behesht-i Ma'sumeh Cemetery in Qum. Allāma Amīnī's second wife passed away in 1376 Sh/ 1988 and is also buried in Qum.

Allāma Amīnī often expressed his warm appreciation to both of his wives for their sacrifice and contentment. It was through their support that he was able to undertake the research necessary for *al-Ghadīr* and his other great works of scholarship.

Sheikh Aḥmad, his eldest son from his second wife, pursued religious education both in Tehran and then in Qum, where he has now lived for over thirty years. He regularly travels to Najaf to oversee the running of the Imam Amīr al-Mu'minīn Public Library in the post-Saddam era. Dr. Muḥammad, the younger brother of Sheikh Aḥmad, is a university professor in Islamic History and lives in Tehran.

Amīnī has come!

Sayyid Muḥammad-Taqī Baḥr al-'Ulūm[1] a renowned Najafi scholar, reported that some time after the death of Allāma Amīnī he wondered about the reward of the profound devotion and scholarship showcased in *al-Ghadīr*. One night, he had a dream. He narrates: "It was the Day of Resurrection, and all the Shia *ulema* (religious scholars) were gathered in a single line. One by one, they received a glass of most blessed water from the hands of Imam 'Alī. At the same time, some people shouted, 'Amīnī has come! Amīnī has come!' Imam 'Alī instructed Amīnī to bypass the long line, and to come close to him. When Allāma was close, Imam 'Alī started pouring water on Amīnī with his own hands, instead of giving him a glass of water."

1. d. 1393 AH/ 1973

The Imam Amīr al-Mu'minīn Public Library of Najaf

Ever since Sheikh Muḥammad b. al-Ḥasan al-Ṭūsī[1] was forced to migrate from Baghdad in 447 AH/ 1056, Najaf has been a pre-eminent centre of Shia learning.[2] In the medieval times, there was a library in the precincts of Imam 'Alī's shrine, but its manuscripts became scattered through the years. In Allāma Amīnī's day, with the exception of a few private libraries belonging to notable religious scholars, there was no public library of distinction in the city. The only public library that could be found in the city belonged to the *ḥusayniyyah* of the pilgrims from Shushtar; it amounted to no more than a 4 by 5 metre room, and was managed by a gentleman whose time was largely devoted to other things.[3]

The fact that Najaf did not have a prestigious and outstanding public library to match its status as a nine-hundred-year-old centre for learning did not sit well with Allāma Amīnī, particularly due to his acquaintance with numerous great and prominent libraries around the world. And so, he

1. 385-460 AH/ 995-1067

2. For a short biography of the Sheikh al-Ṭūsī, see, Abū Ja'far Muḥammad b. al-Ḥasan b. 'Alī "al-Ṭūsī", *al-Nihayah: A Concise Description of Islamic Laws and Legal Opinions*, trans. A. Ezzati (London, 2008), pp. i-iv; and Ayatollah Āqā Buzurg al-Ṭihrānī, "Ḥayāt al-Sheikh al-Ṭūsī," in *al-Tibyān fī tafsīr al-Qur'ān*, 10 vols. (Najaf, 1376 AH/ 1956; Beirut, n.d.), vol. 1, pp. i-lxxiv; ed. Aḥmad Ḥabīb Qaṣīr al-'Āmilī, 10 vols. (Beirut, 1431 AH/ 2010), vol. 1, pp. 5-74.

3. There is a mention of a certain "Al-Hussainiyah Library, Najef" in *The Middle East*, 4th edn. (London, 1955), p. 143, which seems to be the same "private" library listed in the chapter devoted to Iraq.

established a public library in the city, and named it after Najaf's most well-known inhabitant, Imam 'Alī, the Prince of the Faithful. He announced the building project on the 1st of Jamadi al-Awwal 1373 AH/ 1953, and planned to locate it in the al-Ḥuwaysh district. With its learned residents and *madrasas*, al-Ḥuwaysh is the religious scholars' quarter of Najaf, and a five-minute walk southern gate of Imam 'Alī's holy shrine.

The Imam Amīr al-Mu'minīn Public Library was established through the support of the devotees of Imam 'Alī, mainly wealthy Iranian merchants from Tabriz, Tehran, Isfahan, and Mashhad, whose names and contributions have been recorded in the library's founding documents. The substantial funding made it possible to purchase a piece of land of 260 square metres adjacent to the *madrasas* of the Qazwīnis, the Bukhārīs, the Sharabīyānīs, and the Īrawānīs, as well as those of Grand Ayatollah Sayyid Muḥammad-Kāẓim Ṭabāṭabā'ī-Yazdī, and Ayatollah Muḥammad-Kāẓim Khurāsānī. The land had originally belonged to a Baghdad-based attorney at law, Ḥamzah Baḥr, and was large enough to accommodate a building of three floors and a basement. The Imam Amīr al-Mu'minīn Public Library was officially opened on the anniversary of the event of Ghadīr Khumm in 1379 AH/ 1959. The opening event was attended by many local dignitaries. At a later point, the library was expanded through the purchase of 430 square metres of a neighbouring piece of land from the Rafī'ī Sayyid family.

Allāma Amīnī's vision for the library was that it should provide various facilities and services for its users, ranging from study rooms to refreshments. The library was also to accommodate research projects, and provide services to other Iraqi libraries. Today, the basement of the library houses manuscripts in a unit which protects the library's collection from physical deterioration. On the ground floor, one can find the information desk, the main stacks of printed books and a large reading hall. The first floor is devoted to stacks of the donated books, administrative offices, and a private reading hall for ladies. The second floor of the library, still under construction, has been devoted to a computer room, digital library, accounts department, and archived storage.

On the inauguration day of the Imam Amīr al-Mu'minīn Public Library, the late Ayatollah Sheikh Āqā Buzurg Ṭihrānī remarked to Allāma Amīnī that upon stepping inside the library, he had experienced a special feeling inspiring him to prostrate in gratitude to Allah for the blessing of having had such a library in Najaf. This remark sufficiently portrays the status of the library in the eyes of the dignitaries of Najaf.

Allāma Amīnī at Imam Amīr al-Mu'minīn Public Library, Najaf

The founding collection of the Imam Amīr al-Mu'minīn Public Library consisted of the same works that Allāma Amīnī would have referred to for *al-Ghadīr*. Many individuals facilitated the growth of the library's collections, especially Allāma Amīnī's sons, Sheikh Riḍā and Dr. Muḥammad-Hādī, who donated their own personal collections. Many other notable individuals donated materials and books to the library in its first year[1] contributing to the rich and vast collection. In addition to these clerics, numerous university academics also donated books and research materials to the library[2].

In terms of financial support, the library benefited from the help of a number of merchants active in Iran, Iraq, Syria, and some European countries[3].

1. There are many other notable individuals who donated materials and books to the library in its first year. Some of them are as follows: Ayatollah Sayyid Shahāb al-Dīn Mar'ashī Najafī, Mirza Ibrāhīm Amīnī, Sheikh Asad Ḥaydar, Ayatollah Sheikh Mirza 'Alī Zanjānī, Sayyid Naṣr Allāh Jazāyirī, the late Ayatollah Sayyid 'Abd al-'Azīz Ṭabāṭabā'ī-Yazdī, Sheikh Asad Ḥaydar al-Najafī, Sheikh 'Alī Ākhūndī, Sheikh Muḥammad Ākhūndī, Ayatollah Sheikh Āqā Buzurg Ṭihrānī, Ayatollah Sayyid 'Abd al-Hādī Shīrāzī, Grand Ayatollah Sayyid Abū al-Qāsim Mūsawī Khu'ī, Sayyid Aḥmad Ṭāliqānī, Ayatollah Muḥammad-Taqī Ja'farī, Sayyid Murtaḍā Mustajābī, Sheikh Ḥasan al-Zayn, Sayyid Mūsā Ṣadr, Grand Ayatollah Sayyid Muḥsin al-Ḥakīm, Sayyid Muḥammad-Mahdī al-Mūsawī al-Khirsān, Sayyid Muḥammad-Bāqir al-Mūsawī al-Khirsān, and Sayyid Ḥasan al-Amīn.

2. Dr. Ḥusayn 'Alī Maḥfūẓ of Baghdad, Dr. Muḥammad-Riḍā Bānkī Tihrānī, Dr. 'Abd al-Bāqī Gulpinarli, Ṣalāḥ al-Dīn al-Munajjid, Sayyid Qudrat Allāh Shāhmurādī, Dr. Ḥasan Faḍā'ilī, Dr. Ṣādiq Riḍāzādih Shafaq, 'Ārif Salīm Qizilughli, and Dr. Sayyid Riḍā Mu'addab. Other founding donors include Field Marshal 'Azīz-Allāh Khan Ḍarghāmī, an Iranian army officer, and in recent years the present author.

3. Such merchants included Sayyid Riḍā Taqawī, Ismā'īl Sīgārī, Sayyid 'Abd al-Mahdī Āl Ṭu'mah Mūsawī, Muḥammad 'Alī Labīb Tabrīzī, Taqī Barq Lāmi' Tabrīzī (all from Iran), 'Alī Zāyir Ḥasan (from Kuwait), and 'Abd al-Jalīl Ismā'īl Sārah and Ḥusayn al-Shākirī (both from Iraq).

Throughout its history, the Imam Amīr al-Mu'minīn Public Library regularly received books from prominent Sunni scholars.[1] In addition, the library receives donations and gifts from academic and cultural organizations.[2]

By the end of 1382 AH/ 1962, just ten years after its establishment, the library had received 10,504 volumes of books in Arabic, 6,815 volumes in Persian, 481 volumes in French, 382 volumes in Turkish, 305 volumes in Urdu, 248 volumes in English, 21 volumes in Armenian, and 4 volumes in Spanish. It also received 1,485 manuscripts in Arabic, and 711 manuscripts in Persian. The library's total holdings, therefore, amounted to 20,956 volumes.

The Imam Amīr al-Mu'minīn Public Library is a place where the contributions of other Muslim societies can be discovered, the library itself has made an immense contribution to the scholarly and cultural atmosphere of Najaf by providing inspiration for the many other public libraries to be built in the city. It has also inspired innovative research throughout Iraq by attracting international researchers to

1. Such as Muḥammad 'Abd al-Ghanī Ḥasan, Aḥmad Khayrī al-Ḥanafī, 'Āyishah Bint al-Shāṭī, 'Abd al-Raḥmān al-Kayyālī, Usāmah Nāṣir al-Naqshbandī, and 'Ādil Shujā' al-Dimashqī.

2. The long list of the library's institutional donors includes the University of Oxford; Oxford University Press; the American University of Beirut; the Iraqi Ministry of Culture; the University of Baghdad; the Cutural Section of the German Democratic Republic in Baghdad; Yale University Press; the University of Tehran; the Iraqi Academy of Arabic Literature, Baghdad; the Pahlawī Foundation, Tehran; the Iranian Archeological Society; al-Jumhurīyyah Library, Baghdad; University of Mosul; al-Mustansariyyah University, Baghdad; the Cultural Section of the Saudi Embassy, Baghdad; the Kuwaiti Institute of Manuscripts; Book Translation and Distribution Agency, Tehran; Suleimaniah Library, Turkey; the Library of Congress, New York; the Geographical Center, Beirut; the Iran Cultural Institute, Tehran; the Cultural Center of India, Baghdad; and the Afghan embassy in Baghdad.

Najaf, and inviting them to witness the special religious and scholarly atmosphere of the city[1].

The story of the Imam Amīr al-Mu'minīn Public Library deserves a separate book, and it all began with Allāma Amīnī who both founded the library and oversaw its running. According to Sheikh Aḥmad Amīnī, Sheikh Riḍā Amīnī used to be the library's acting director and curator even in the lifetime of Allāma for around 20 years. As per the will of Allāma Amīnī and his official letter of endowment, his son Sheikh Riḍā was not only the second persona on the board of trustees but also the head of the library. Many noteworthy achievements were obtained due to Sheikh Riḍā's management. After Allāma's death, Sheikh Riḍā was responsible for the library's future development. His task was made more difficult by the ex-Baathists' purge of Iranian nationals in 1354 Sh/ 1975.

After Sheikh Riḍā was returned to Iran, he settled in Tehran. He no longer had any direct connection to the li-

1. Among the leading scholars and dignitaries who are indicated in the records of the Library the following can be mentioned: Dr. Sayyid Zawwār Ḥusayn Zaydī of the University of Lahore; 'Abbās Ārām, the former Minister of Foreign Affairs, Iran; Dr. Maḥmūd Yūnus of the University of Jakarta; the Indonesian ambassador in Iraq; Muḥammad As'ad Ṣafar Kamāl, the Indonesian cultural attache in Cairo; Jalāl al-Dīn Mallāḥ, the curator of the Aleppo branch of the Syrian National Library; Dr. Ṣalāḥ al-Dīn al-Munajjid; Dr. Aḥmad Farhād, former rector of the University of Tehran; Dr. Tafaḍḍulī, the former curator of the Library of the National Parliament of Iran; Sayyid Fānī, the cultural attache of India in Baghdad; Dr. Ḥusayn 'Alī Maḥfūẓ of the University of Baghdad; Sayyid Muḥammad-Ṣādiq Baḥr al-'Ulūm; Dr. Maḥmūd Shahābī of the University of Tehran; Ayatollah Nāṣir Makārim-Shīrāzī; Ayatollah Ja'far Subḥānī Tabrīzī; Dr. Otto Schelin, Copenhagen; Dr. Jacques Waardenburg, then of Montreal, Canada; Prof. William Montgomery Watt, Scotland; Robert Cote, USA; Sayyid 'Alī Ẓahīr, India; and Muḥammad Hidāyatī, Cairo.

brary in Najaf. Instead, the library was under the direction of the bureau (*bayt)* of the late Grand Ayatollah Sayyid Abū al-Qāsim Musawī Khu'ī for several years until his death. After Ayatollah Khu'ī, the bureau of Grand Ayatollah Sayyid 'Alī Ḥusaynī Sīstānī continued directing the library. The latter then appointed Hajj Mu'īn Jiddī Zaynī, a merchant in Najaf. It was in 2006, after the downfall of Saddam Hussein, (in 2003) that Grand Ayatollah Sīstānī asked Sheikh Riḍā to return to Najaf. Skeikh Riḍā then called on a team, comprising his two brothers (Sheikh Aḥmad and Dr. Muḥammad) as well as his nephew, Dr. 'Abbās Ākhūndī (a former Iranian minister of Roads and Urban Planning), to go to Najaf to direct the library's management. They met with Ayatollah Sīstānī, who requested them to take hold of the Library to run it anew. Clearly, the downfall of Saddam Hussein's rule in 2003 marked a new phase in the history of the library. In this post-Saddam, relatively free era, the two younger sons of Allāma Amīnī, particularly Sheikh Aḥmad, could travel to Najaf to supervise its management.

Allāma Amīnī's Students and Followers

Great people usually inspire others, the late Allāma 'Abd al-Ḥusayn Amīnī was no exception. When interacting with his peers, colleagues, classmates, and students they would notice his exceptional character, methods of teaching, research practices, and exemplary religious piety. He taught for a relatively short period in his hometown of Tabriz. Other than that, upon request, he sometimes delivered speeches at mosques. He gave religious lectures in Kermanshah and Mashhad for ten days in 1365 AH/ 1945 and 1338 Sh/ 1959 respectively, and in Isfahan during 1376 AH/ 1956 and 1338 Sh/ 1959. The reason for his limited preaching was simply that his *al-Ghadīr* project took the majority of his time. However, he willingly gave his expert views to those who sought them, regardless of whether or not the enquirer was a cleric. What follows is just a small collection of those who were influenced by Allāma.

Sheikh Asad Ḥaydar al-Najafī

Allāma Amīnī inspired others to undertake great projects in which historical background and causes of events were derived from authentic sources. Once, the late Shia Iraqi scholar Sheikh Asad Ḥaydar al-Najafī[1] met with Allāma Amīnī and sought guidance on developing an article on the life and times of the sixth Infallible Imam Ja'far al-Ṣādiq to be sent to a periodical published in Baghdad. Allāma Amīnī strongly advised him against writing something superficial out of obligation in order to fill a few pages with commonly-related accounts. He said the status of Imam Ja'far al-

1. d. 1405 AH/ 1984

Ṣādiq is so high that a shallow piece for a transitory end was unacceptable. Instead, Allāma suggested that he conduct an authentic study which communicates aspects of the Imam's graceful life. The impact of this advice can be clearway seen in the six-volume series *al-Imam al-Ṣādiq wa al-madhāhib al-arba'ah*, written by Sheikh Asad Ḥaydar al-Najafī. (6 vols. in 3, 1375 AH/ 1959; 2nd edn., Beirut, 1390 AH/ 1969).

Sheikh Muḥammad Mahdī Shams al-Dīn

The late Sheikh Muḥammad Mahdī Shams al-Dīn[1] was a renowned Lebanese Shia scholar whose books, especially those in the realm of Shia history, showcase the extent to which he was influenced by Allāma Amīnī. In particular, the Amīnī outlook is recognizable in Shams al-Dīn's approach toward the history of the tragedy of Karbala , and his critical approach to ancient sources.

Dr. Syed Husain Mohammad Jafri

In Pakistan, Dr. Syed Husain Mohammad Jafri[2] was influenced by Allāma Amīnī's views of early Islamic history. This is evident in his book *The Origins and Early Development of Shi`a Islam* (London/ Beirut, 1979; Karachi/ Oxford, 2000). In it, Syed Jafri attempts to trace back major events through the ancient texts concerned.

Prof. Dr. Sayyid Sadiq Naqvi

In 2007 when the present author went to India to research the impact of Ashura on English literature, he had the opportunity to meet with Prof. Dr. Sayyid Sadiq Naqvi[3]

1. d. 2001
2. d. 2019
3. d. 2017

of Hyderabad, Andhra Pradesh, India. Prof. Naqvi remarked that as a student, he had taken lessons in Islamic history from the late Allāma Amīnī, during the time he was there using the rich Indian libraries.

Prof. Dr. Ṣafā ʻAbd al-ʻAzīz Khulūsī

Prof. Dr. Ṣafā ʻAbd al-ʻAzīz Khulūsī (commonly spelled as Khulusi) (1917- *ca.* 1996) was a scholar who played a key role in the formation of new Iraqi Shia madrasas at Najaf.[1] In addition to translating the first volume of *al-Ghadīr* into English, he wrote his PhD dissertation at the University of London on the title "Shiism and its Influence on Arabic Literature" (1947); indicating the impression Allāma Amīnī had made on him.

Ayatollah Muḥammad-Ṣādiq Najmī

In the summer of 1388 AH/ 1968, Allāma Amīnī spent around three weeks in the village of Sharafkhānih, near the lake Urmia in the West Azerbaijan Province, Northwest Iran, to benefit from the mineral water of the region for medical purposes. As luck would have it, Ayatollah Muḥammad-Ṣādiq Najmī (who was then a student of Islamic studies in Qum) was spending his summer holiday in the same village as Allāma Amīnī. According to Ayatollah Najmī, Allāma Amīnī used to stay in the same house as him; Allāma on the ground floor, and the Ayatollah Najmī on the upper floor. Every day, at around 10 a.m., Ayatollah Najmī prepared a breakfast for Allāma Amīnī. During and after

1. See Nakash, *The Shi'is of Iraq* (Princeton, N.J., 1995; 2003), p. 262. Parenthetically, Dr. Khulusi was an active Arab academic; this is evident from the range of books he authored and the Oxford teams of Arabic dictionaries in which he participated. His translation textbook, *Fann al-tarjimah* [The Craft of Translation] (Baghdad, 1956) is still reprinted in Arab countries.

breakfast, the two had very fruitful scholarly dialogues. Ayatollah Najmī seized the opportunity to learn from the wealth of experience Allāma Amīnī had gained throughout his *al-Ghadīr* research. Ayatollah Najmī who had long been focusing on certain seminal Sunnite hadith collections such as *Ṣaḥīḥ al-Bukhārī* and *Ṣaḥīḥ Muslim*, showed his notes to Allāma Amīnī. This exchange proved beneficial as Allāma Amīnī gave Ayatollah Najmi plenty of additional research avenues. Later, Ayatollah Najmī published two important books; *Siyrī dar ṣaḥīḥayn* which is a critical appraisal of both *Ṣaḥīḥ al-Bukhārī* and *Ṣaḥīḥ Muslim*, and *Sukhanān-i Ḥusayn b. 'Alī az Madīneh tā Karbalā*, a collection of Imam al-Ḥusayn's discourses from the moment he left Medina up to the moment of his tragic but triumphant martyrdom at Karbala.[1]

Ayatollah Muḥammad-Bāqir Maḥmūdī

The late Ayatollah Muḥammad-Bāqir Maḥmūdī[2] was another researcher who benefited from Allāma Amīnī's guidance and the library in Najaf. While Ayatollah Maḥmūdī was in Najaf, he was concerned with producing critical, annotated, and definitive editions of authentic accounts of Islamic history, mainly based on certain authoritative Sunni textbooks and references. For this purpose, he used to visit the Imam Amīr al-Mu'minīn Public Library that Allāma Amīnī established at Najaf. Both the library and its founder proved of immense help, a fact often asserted by Ayatollah Maḥmūdī.

1. The present author translated the latter from Persian into English, titled *From Medina to Karbala in the Words of Imam al-Ḥusayn*, published by Sun Behind the Cloud Publications (Birmingham, 2012; 2nd edn., 2013).

2. d. 1427 AH/ 2006

Ayatollah Sayyid 'Abd al-'Azīz Ṭabāṭabā'ī Yazdī

Known to be a leading scholar, Ayatollah Sayyid 'Abd al-'Azīz Ṭabāṭabā'ī Yazdī[1] was the great-grandson of Grand Ayatollah Sayyid Muḥammad-Kāẓim Ṭabāṭabā'ī Yazdī[2] and gained much from his interaction with Allāma Amīnī. He used to assist with and receive lessons from two great Najaf-based, Iranian scholars; the late Sheikh Āqā Buzurg Ṭihrānī[3] whose voluminous work *al-Dharī'ah ilā taṣānīf al-Shī'ah* has been an unsurpassed bibliography, and the late Allāma Amīnī. The influence of Allāma Amīnī is discernible in the array of research projects Ayatollah Sayyid 'Abd al-'Azīz Ṭabāṭabā'ī Yazdī has completed. In line with Allāma Amīnī's *al-Ghadīr*, he produced a book named *al-Ghadīr fī al-turāth al-Islāmī* (Beirut, 1414 AH/ 1993; 2nd edn., Qum, 1415 AH/ 1374 Sh/ 1996); *Qabasāt min faḍā'il Amīr al-Mu'minīn* (2nd edn., Qum, 1421 AH/ 2000); an edition of *Faḍā'il Amīr al-Mu'minīn* 'Alī *b. Abī Ṭālib* of Aḥmad b. Ḥanbal (Qum, 1433 AH/ 2011); and *Dastnewishā-yi bidast āmadih az Nahj al-Balāghah tā pāyān-i sadih-yi dahum-i hijrī* (Tehran, 1379 Sh/ 2000). In addition to the above works, there are many other works of his that are still in manuscript form, such as, "'Alā ḍifāf al-Ghadīr", "Min fayḍ al-Ghadīr", his notes on *al-Ghadīr*, and "*Inbā' al-samā' birazīyyah Karbalā*", this last one is particularly an extended version of the second part of Allāma's book *Sīratunā wa sunnatunā* which concerns Prophet Muḥammad's tearful anticipation of Imam al-Ḥusayn's martyrdom. It deserves mention that some of his scholarly annotations on the first four volumes of *al-Ghadīr* have appeared in its reprint edition produced at the Institute of Islamic Fiqh in Qum.

1. d. 1374 Sh/ 1996

2. d. 1337 AH/ 1918

3. d. 1389 AH/ 1969

Ayatollah 'Azīz-Allāh 'Uṭāridī

The late Ayatollah 'Azīz-Allāh 'Uṭāridī[1] was a renowned scholar in the fields of Islamic history and archaeology, hadith and hadith-based literature, and lexicological studies. When he met Allāma Amīnī in Najaf, Allāma often suggested that he translate certain books from Arabic into Persian, including al-'Alawī al-Ḥaḍaramī's insightful volume *al-Naṣā'iḥ al-kāfiyah liman yatawallā Mu'āwīyah*, and Allāma Muḥammad-Ḥusayn Kāshif al-Ghiṭā's *al-Arḍ wa al-turbah al-Ḥusaynīyyah*. The latter was a slim but influential treatise on the reasons for prostrating in prayer on the soil of Karbala; a highly-recommended act due to the association of the soil of Karbala with Imam al-Ḥusayn's martyrdom. Ayatollah 'Uṭāridī also received some insightful guidance from Allāma Amīnī when he was developing a concise compilation of the Arabic lexicon *Tāj al-'arūs min jawāhir al-qāmūs*, originally written by the Cairo-based linguist and lexicographer Sayyid Muḥammad Murtaḍā al-Ḥusaynī al-Zabīdī[2].

Sheikh Muḥammad-Riḍā Ja'farī

Ayatollah Sheikh Muḥammad-Riḍā Ja'farī[3] is known for writing an English translation of *Uṣūl al-kāfi* by the late Sheikh Muḥammad b. Ya'qūb al-Kulaynī.[4] A distinguished disciple of the Najaf-based Grand Ayatollah Sayyid Abū al-Qāsim Mūsawī Khu'ī,[5] the late Ayatollah Ja'farī was also a research assistant to the late Allāma Amīnī when he was

1. d. 1393 Sh/ 2014
2. d. 816 or 817 AH/ 1413 or 1414
3. d. 1389 Sh/ 2010
4. d. 329 AH/ 941
5. d. 1413 AH/ 1992

developing *al-Ghadīr*. He often indicated that his combined Qur'anic and historical approaches to the Islamic articles of faith including the principle of Imamate was heavily influenced by Allāma Amīnī's approach.[1] Likely as a result of Allāma's suggestions, the late Ayatollah Ja'farī studied English to the degree that he secured the role of Kuala-Lumpur based deputy to the late Ayatollah Khu'ī, and also translated *Nahj al-Balāghah* into English.

Sheikh Bāqir b. Sharīf al-Qarashī

The great Shia Iraqi historian, Sheikh Bāqir b. Sharīf al-Qarashī[2] was one of the outstanding personalities who received much inspiration from Allāma Amīnī and benefited greatly from the Imam Amīr al-Mu'minīn Public Library of Najaf. Allāma Amīnī's method of adopting a combined historical and doctrinal approach can be easily observed in the wide and influential range of Shia historical texts he developed. This range included three volumes on the life of Prophet Muḥammad and 24 volumes on the lives and times of the rest of the Infallibles. His book on the life of Imam al-Ḥusayn is also available in three substantial volumes.

Ayatollah Sayyid Murtaḍā Nujūmī

It was as a result of attending the lectures of Allāma Amīnī in Kermanshah that Ayatollah Sayyid Murtaḍā Nujūmī[3] decided to continue his education, and went to Najaf for advanced Shia Islamic studies.

1. See Aḥmad Amīnī, "Dar hadīth-i dīgarān," in *Nādirah-yi dowrān: Yād nāmih-yi Marḥūm Ayatollah Allāma Sheikh Muḥammad-Riḍā Ja'farī*, ed. Sayyid Ḥusayn Ḥā'irī (Qum, 1389 Sh/ 2011), p. 63.

2. 1344-1433 AH/ 1923-2012

3. d. 1388 Sh/ 2009

Ayatollah Sayyid Ghulām Riḍā Kasā'ī

The late Ayatollah Sayyid Ghulām Riḍā Kasā'ī[1] was a brother-in-law of Allāma Amīnī. An accomplished scholar, he was respected by Allāma Amīnī. Since he was often a research assistant to Allāma, including in his research expedition to India, he took the opportunity and accomplished his own research activities concerned with the merits and virtues of the daughter of Prophet Muḥammad, Fāṭimah al-Zahrā. His book, *Manāqib al-Zahrā* (Qum, 1398 AH/ 1978) was published posthumously by his wife.

1. d. 1394 AH/ 1974

Please Pray for My Son

Once when Allāma Amīnī was resident in Najaf, a son of a certain Sunnite Iraqi Prime Minister (during the reign of Aḥmad Ḥasan al-Bakr[1]) had a serious illness for which doctors, neither in Iraq nor abroad, could do anything. At the suggestion of a Shia employee of his office, the bewildered Iraqi prime minister wrote a short note to Allāma Amīnī in which he asked Allāma to pray for his son's recovery. Allāma Amīnī wrote back, saying his son would recover thanks to the graceful attention of Imam 'Alī. That night, as Allāma Amīnī stood at the gates of Imam 'Alī's Sacred Sanctuary, two figures approached him. The Iraqi prime minister and his recovered son were on their way to thank him.

1. d. 1982 [r. 1968-1979]

Ghadīr-centered Study Circles

Allāma Amīnī was passionate about conveying true and pure Islamic teachings through his lectures and writings. Although developing *al-Ghadīr* took most of his attention for at least 40 years, he sometimes accepted requests to deliver occasional lectures. From time to time, he also ran some Ghadīr-centered study circles in Mashhad and Tehran. Similar circles were formed in Isfahan and Tabriz, too. In Mashhad, a number of school and university teachers attended, and the outcome of their discussions later on appeared in the form of the book *Ḥassāstarīn farāz-i tārīkh yā dāstān-i Ghadīr* (Mashhad, 1960, with subsequent reprint editions). The late Dr. Sayyid 'Alī-Akbar Majīdī-Fayyāḍ[1], then the dean of the Faculty of Letters and the Humanities of the Firdowsī University of Mashhad, wrote a preface to the volume.

At these study circles, *al-Ghadīr* was taught, and its contents formed the basis of these lessons in Islamic studies in Tehran. Late Ayatollah Riḍā Amīnī used to teach *al-Ghadīr* in Tehran around 1987-1989. This private class had two diligent students: Sheikh Aḥmad and Dr. Muḥammad Amīnī. Later on, between 1994-95, Sheikh Aḥmad taught *al-Ghadīr* in Tehran on weekends.

Quite recently, that is from 3 December 2018, Sheikh Aḥmad Amīnī has started teaching a private lesson of *al-Ghadīr* at home in Qum. It is held three days a week, often in the evening of Saturday, Monday, and Wednesday. The present author regularly attends these insightful and thought-provoking lectures which shed light on doctrinal

1. 1898-1971

aspects of Islamic history that are seldom discussed anywhere else. Approximately ten clerics often attend the lessons and raise questions that turn into fruitful discussions with Sheikh Aḥmad Amīnī.

Outside Iran, these study circles used to be formed by Hajj Muḥammad Jamāl in Muscat, Oman and by Hajj Muḥammad Ja'far Khujah in Zanzibar, Tanzania. In Syria, Sheikh Muḥammad Mar'ī and his brother Sheikh Aḥmad Mar'ī in Aleppo, ran such circles. In Faw'ah of Idlib, Hajj Rashīd al-Faw'ānī used to teach lessons from *al-Ghadīr.*

It must be emphasized that the works of Allāma Amīnī need to be viewed within the framework of the socio-political and intellectual circumstances in which he lived. The effect of upheavals in Iran, Iraq, and the countries he travelled to, must be taken into account when examining development of the works he devoted his energy to.

A Clarification

Soon after the 1979 Iranian revolution, many people and political parties claimed that they had played some role in developing the revolution, hence claiming their share in the new administration. One of such group was the small band of bazaar-oriented merchants known as "Co-affiliated Islamic associations" and a militant group known as "the Devotees of Islam" who might still take pride in its founders, and particularly Sayyid Mujtabā Navvāb-Ṣafavī[1], who influenced them to kill the statesmen of the ex-Pahlavī regime in Iran. Much earlier, he attempted to kill the Iranian historian Aḥmad Kasravī on 21 April 1945; however, later, he declared on 20 February 1946 that he was resolute to kill him for his writings that sounded against Islamic main-

1. Executed in Tehran on 18 January 1956

stream, an accusation that Kasravī never accepted. In effect of such purely political inspiration and impetus, Sayyid Moḥammad 'Alī and Sayyid Ḥusayn Imāmī assassinated Aḥmad Kasravī at a judicial court in Tehran on 20 February 1946. Much later, Moḥammad Bukhārāyī[1] assassinated the Pahlavī regime's prime minister Hassan 'Alī Manṣūr in front of the parliament in Tehran on 21st January 1965.

After the Iranian revolution, Navvāb-Ṣafavī's wife, Mrs. Nayyirih Sādāt Iḥtishām Razavī, in an interview with the Iranian weekly Soroush[2], claimed that it was Allāma Amīnī, with certain Najaf-based leading ayatollahs, who had issued a fatwa in that such an assassination, particularly that of Aḥmad Kasravī, was religiously legal, hence permissible and executable. After some time, this claim was expressly refuted outright. Similar claims were made that Allāma Amīnī had supported certain Iranian or Middle-Eastern political-minded clerics, particularly when they had to stay outside Iran. Such claims are absolutely false and baseless. They never gain any merit or virtue for Allāma Amīnī, either. In fact, when Sayyid Mujtabā Navvāb-Ṣafavī went to Najaf 1944, just at the age of 19, several mujtahids recommended him to study there; however, politically-inspired, he preferred to return to Iran for political activities. Allāma Amīnī never instigated him to assassinate anybody; instead, he advised Navvāb-Ṣafavī to remain in Najaf and study to become a scholar. However, he was inspired to be a political and militant activist. Navvāb Ṣafavī never continued his lessons in Najaf. Similar claims are made that the armed group The Devotees of Islam had got the consent and fatwa of the late Ayatollah Sayyid Muḥammad-Hādī Milānī to embark on killing statesmen and intellectuals whose apparent ges-

1. Executed in Tehran onn16 June 1965

2. No. 130, dated 16 January 1982

tures might sometimes be interpreted as their opposition against Islam. Later Ayatollah Sayyid 'Alī Milānī refuted such a false claim and showed that those militant groups never sought such a *fatwa* from the late Ayatollah Sayyid Moḥammad-Hadī Milānī. It was Mr. 'Alī Amīnī Najafī, a grandson of Allāma Amīnī, who published a note in Persian on the website of the BBC on 12 March 2012 in this regard.[1]

1. For more information in Persian see http://bbc.com/persian/iran/2012/03/120313_144_kasravi_amini_murder#orb-banner.

Horizons for Further Scholarship

Sadly, Allāma Amīnī has not been mentioned in the outstanding English encyclopedias[1] and dictionaries[2] devoted to the Muslim world. Apart from the relatively short entry contributed by Dr. H. Algar to the *Encyclopaedia Irannica*, there is little mention in the broad field of contemporary Islamic studies.

Some interesting ideas for further research into the life and times of Allāma Amīnī are listed below.

What were the family and cultural values which enabled Allāma Amīnī's family to safeguard their staunch religious values? No doubt, mere religious passion and sentiment never prove powerful enough to withstand a globally strong secular and at times atheistic schools of thought. In what manner was Allāma Amīnī educated, both at home and in the madrasah? Will it be feasible for other conscientious Muslims to protect their children in the same manner?

While it is known that the madrasah-based education Allāma Amīnī received played a key role in prompting him to develop his works, we might question whether it is feasible to reconstruct the same religious atmosphere to educate more figures like Allāma Amīnī? If so, what developments may be necessary to consider? Which obstacles are there?

1. For instance, there is not an article on Allama Amīnī in *The Encyclopaedia of Islam*, 2nd edn., and J. L. Esposito, ed., *The Oxford Encyclopedia of the Modern Islamic World* (4 vols., New York, 1995).

2. There is no entry devoted to Allama Amīnī in such dictionaries as E. Van Donzel, ed., *Islamic Desk Reference, Compiled from the Encyclopaedia of Islam* (Leiden, 1994), and J. L. Esposito, ed., *The Oxford Dictionary of Islam* (New York, 2003).

With regard to the works of Allāma Amīnī, both published and in manuscript, due attention must be paid to *al-Ghadīr*, especially the remaining nine volumes that have not been published. Even within *al-Ghadīr*, further research projects must be devoted to its internal structure. What are the main research methodologies of Allāma Amīnī in *al-Ghadīr*, especially when compared with his other works references? As a Qur'an interpreter, did he apply the same hermeneutical strategies to interpret the hadiths he relied on? What are the common denominators and differences between Allāma Amīnī's historical scholarship and his literary interpretation? What were his yardsticks used to measure whether or not a Sunni hadith was reliable enough to base his inferences on? Is it feasible for other scholars to utilize, and even develop, his research methodologies in other branches of Islamic scholarship, such as Qur'anic studies? Can these research methods and strategies be taught? What are the limitations and shortcomings of the research methods and strategies he used, particularly in contrast to modern developments?

Which components of Islamic literature did Allāma Amīnī consider? How did he judge a poem to be worthy of being included in the Ghadīr-oriented literature? Can his historical and doctrinal standards be applied to other branches of Islamic literature, such as Ḥusayni literature, particularly the ones based on Ashura? In contrast to Marxist notions of 'the literature of commitment', as developed and promoted by Theodore Adorno and Jean-Paul Sartre, and those of 'party literature', as touched upon in Lenin's works, what are the requirements of a purely and precisely 'Islamic' literature? Can one extract and develop a framework, and ideally a theory of Islamic literature of commitment based on Allāma Amīnī's works? What are the mutual relationships between history and literature, as highlighted in the poems included in *al-Ghadīr*? In what respects are Allāma Amīnī's historical concerns different from those of the contemporary American literary scholar Haden White? The Italian literary critic Italo Calvino delineated several outstanding features of classics. Can one come up with a parallel outline based on Allāma Amīnī's literary measures? What are the historical and doctrinal responsibilities of a devout Muslim man of letters? Based on *al-Ghadīr*, in what respect is Islamic literature different from Muslim literature?

In addition to Allāma Amīnī's works, the library he established in Najaf deserves several separate studies. What were the effects of his Library on other libraries in Iraq? Which international libraries inspired Allāma's public library in Najaf? What are the historical stages of the library in Najaf? The late Dr. Muḥammad-Hādī Amīnī believed that the establishment of the library created new literary and scholarly trends at Najaf; what were these effects and trends? Which people and works have appeared in effect of the presence of the Library in Najaf? Was there any trace of the effects of the Library in Najaf on the religio-scholarly atmosphere at Karbala?

In the realm of translation, which corrections did Allāma Amīnī make to the volumes Wāḥidī translated from the Arabic into Persian? Why did Allāma Amīnī reject translations carried out by others? What explanation did Allāma Amīnī add to the Persian translations of his works? What suggestions did he accept in the realm of translation? Did Allāma Amīnī translate any piece from Arabic into Persian, and vice versa? If so, how did he go about it? What are probable obstacles for translating Allama Amini's works, particularly *al-Ghadīr*, into other languages, e.g., English, for global readership? Should they be merely translated, or even transcreated (in the sense of the Indian scholar P. Lal's influential framework of transcreation [1972])?

The above questions are intended to prompt the readers to continue research on the legacy of Allāma Amīnī. Certainly answering them would require several volumes and many projects and papers.

In addition to the above, traditional, and rather general biographies must yield their places to academic biographies. Recent trends in biographical scholarship, and particularly the framework of micro-history, must be taken into account; therefore, not only one, but several biographies must be developed for Shia Muslim dignitaries, and in the present case, for Allāma Amīnī. In addition to the above, such modern-trend biographies must be written anew and afresh in other languages, particularly in English, for the benefit of both Muslims and non-Muslims.

Select Bibliography

Works by Allāma Amīnī

Al-Amīnī al-Najafī, 'Abd al-Ḥusayn Aḥmad, *al-Ghadīr fī al-kitāb wa al-sunnah wa al-adab*, 9 vols. (Najaf, 1364-71 AH/ 1945-51).

2nd rev. edn., 11 vols. (Tehran, 1372 AH/ 1952; Beirut, 1387 AH/ 1967.

5th Iranian repr. edn., ed. by Sayyid Maḥmūd al-Hāshimī al-Shāhrūdī, 14 vols. (Qum, 1430 AH/ 1388 Sh/ 2009).

Thamarāt al-asfār ilā al-aqṭār, (originally in 2 volumes) 4 vols. (Qum, 1428-29 AH/ 2007-08).

Sīratunā wa sunnatunā sīrah nabīyyinā wa sunnatih (Najaf, 1384 AH/ 1965; Tehran, 1386 AH/ 1967).

Shuhadā' al-faḍīlah (Najaf, 1355 AH/ 1936; Qum, 1393 AH/ 1352 Sh/ 1973).

Adab al-zā'ir liman yamamm al-Ḥā'ir (Najaf, 1362 AH/ 1943).

Tafsīr Fātiḥah al-Kitāb, ed. Sheikh Riḍā Amīnī (Tehran, 1395 AH/ 1975).

Persian translation by Qudrat Allāh Ḥusaynī Shāhmurādī (2nd edn., Tehran, 1404 AH/ 1983).

Fāṭimah al-Zahrā', ed. Ḥabīb Chāychīyān (Tehran, 1411 AH/ 1990); ed. Dr. Muḥammad Amīnī (Tehran, 1418 AH/ 1997).

al-Maqāsid al-'alīyyah fī al-maṭālib al-sanīyyah, ed. Sayyid Muḥammad Ṭabāṭabāyī Yazdī (Qum, 1434 AH/ 2012).

In addition to the above published works, the following are still in manuscript: "Al-Majālis," a series of lecture notes collected in a series of private lesson on Islamic doctrinal topics; "Al-Asmā' al-ḥusnā" on the honorific designations of Imam 'Alī as indicated in the Holy Qur'an; "I'lām al-anām fī ma'rifah al-Malik al-'allām" a Persian treatise on Islamic monotheism (*al-tawḥīd*); an annotated edition of *Wasā'il al-Shī'ah* of Sheikh al-Ḥurr al-'Āmilī; "Rijāl-i Ādharbāyījān (Azerbaijan)"; a treatise on the book of Sulaym b. Qays al-Hilālī; a treatise on pilgrimage (*ziarat*); a treatise on *dirāyah al-ḥadīth* (hadith evaluation and criticism); a treatise on intent(ion) (*nīyyah*); a treatise on the Qur'anic verse "*wa li-Allāh al-asmā' al-ḥusnā fad'ūhu bihā*" (There are sublime names of Allah; therefore, call on Him by means of them) The Qur'an, Sura al-A'rāf 7:180); "Rīyāḍ al-uns", and "al-'Iṭrah al-ṭāhirah fī al-Kitāb al-'Azīz".

Works about Allāma Amīnī

Abū al-Ḥasanī (Mundhir), 'Alī, "Al-Ghadīr," in *Dānishnāmih-yi Imam 'Alī*, ed. by 'Alī-Akbar Rashād, 12 vols. (Tehran, 1380 Sh/ 2001), vol. 12, pp. 311-376; *Daryā-yi mowj khīz: Zamānih wa kārnāmih-yi 'Allāma Amīnī* (Tehran, 1386 Sh/ 2007).

Al-Amīnī, Muḥammad-Hādī, *Ilā abī* (Najaf, 1390 AH/ 1970). [Classical Arabic elegies in memoriam Allāma Amīnī]

Al-Amīnī al-Najafī, Riḍā, "Ma'a al-kitāb wa al-mu'allif," in *al-Ghadīr fī al-kitāb wa al-sunnah wa al-adab*, by 'Abd al-Ḥusayn Aḥmad al-Amīnī al-Najafī, 2nd rev. edn., 11 vols.

(Tehran, 1372 AH/ 1952; 4th imp., 1396 AH/ 1976), vol. 1, pp. 5-127; esp. pp. 54-125.

Algar, Hamid, "Amīnī, Shaikh 'Abd al-Hosayn" *Encyclopaedia Iranica*, vol. 1 (New York, 1985), pp. 955-56.

Al-Shākirī, *Ḥusayn, Rub' qarn ma'a al-Allāma al-Amīnī* (Qum, 1417 AH/ 1996).

Amīnī-Najafī, Aḥmad, "Dar hadīth-i dīgarān," in *Nādirih-yi dowrān: Yād nāmih-yi Marḥūm Ayatollah Allāma Sheikh Muḥammad-Riḍā Ja'farī*, ed. by Sayyid Ḥusayn Ḥā'irī (Qum, 1389 Sh/ 2011), pp. 61-64.

Amīnī-Najafī, Muḥammad, *Anguīzih-yi dowlathā-yi Umawī wa 'Abbāsi az ja'l wa tarwīj-i ḥikāyat-i izdiwāj-i 'Umar bā Ḥaḍrat-i Umm Kulthūm* (Najaf, 1432 AH/ 2010).

Amīnī, Muḥammad-Hādī, "Majlā-yi fiyḍ-i 'Alī 'alayh al-salām: an interview," *Yādnāmih-yi Allāma Amīnī, Risālat Daily* [Tehran], 1367 Sh/ 1408 AH/ 1988, pp. 3-6.

Baḥr al-'Ulūm, Sayyid Muḥammad-Ṣādiq, "Al-Ḥujjah al-Amīnī," 1392 AH/ 1972; repr. in *Amīn-i sharī'at*, ed. by Sayyid 'Alī Ṭabāṭabā'ī Yazdī (Qum, 1392 Sh/ 2013), pp. 83-158.

Baḥr al-'Ulūm Mīrdāmādī, Sayyid Maḥmūd, *Tu rā salām iy nasīm-i wilāyat: Sharḥ-i ḥāl-i Allāma Amīnī* (Isfahan, 1378 Sh/ 1999).

Dawānī, 'Alī, *Mafākhir-i Islām: Allāma Amīnī*, 2nd edn. (Tehran, 1388 Sh/ 2009), pp. 185-189.

Fakhr-Rohani, Moḥammad-Reza, "Tajrobeh-yeh nevesh-tan-e nokhostin zendeguinameh-ye Allama Amini beh za-ban-e Enguelisi [The experience of writing the first English biography of Allama Amini]", in *Zendeguinameh va khadamat-e elmi va farhangui-ye marhoum Allama Abd al-Husayn Amini/ Biography and Academic Life of Allameh Abdolhossein Amini*, ed. Sadra Sadouqi (Tehran 1398 Sh/ 2019), pp. 137-148.

Iftikhārzādih, Maḥmūd-Riḍā, "Zindiguīnāmih-yi Allāma Amīnī," in *Khulāsih-yi al-Ghadīr*, by Maḥmūd-Riḍā Iftikhārzādih (Tehran, 1380 Sh/ 2001), pp. 21-26.

Gūdarznīyā, Muḥaddithah, *Allāma Amīnī* (Tehran, 1388 Sh/ 2010).

Luṭfī, Mahdī, *Allāma Amīnī: Jur'ah nūsh-i Ghadīr* (Qum, 1379 Sh/ 2000). *Marzbān-i ḥimāsih-yi Ghadīr* (Tabriz, 1383 Sh/ 2004).

Nakha'ī, Farhang, *Yikmāh dar Iṣfahān yā guzārish-i musāfirat-i Allāma-yi Mu'aẓẓam Ḥaḍrat-i Āyatullāh al-'Uẓmā Āqā-yi Ḥāj Sheykh 'Abd al-Ḥusayn Amīnī bih Iṣfahān dar māh-i Ṣafar al-Muẓaffar 1376 Hijrī-yi Qamarī* ([Mashhad], 1367 AH/ 1947).

Qahramānnizhād, Muḥammad, ed., *Marzbān-i ḥimāsih-yi Ghadīr* (Tabriz, 1383 Sh/ 2004).

Sayyid Kubārī, 'Alī-Riḍā, *Allāma Amīnī: Muṣliḥ-i nastūh* (Tehran, 1372 Sh/ 1993).

Subḥānī, Muḥammad Taqī, "Sukhan-i bunyād-i imāmat," in *al-Ghadīr: Ghadīr dar kitāb wa sunnat wa adab*, trans. Sayyid Abū al-Qāsim Ḥusaynī "Zharfā", 12 vols. (Qum, 1397 Sh/ 2018), vol. 1, pp. 3-74. *Yādnāmih-yi Allāma Amīnī wīzhih-yi duwwumīn ijlās-i ḥowzih wa tablīgh*, 2 vols. (Qum, 1379 Sh/ 2000).

Translations of *al-Ghadīr*

Ḥusaynī "Zharfā", Sayyid Abū al-Qāsim, trans., *al-Ghadīr: Ghadīr dar kitāb wa sunnat wa adab*, ed. Sayyid Mahdī Nabawī, 12 vols. (Qum, 1397 Sh/ 1439 AH/ 2018). (In Persian)

Wāḥidī, Sayyid Muḥammad-Taqī, trans., *al-Ghadīr*, by 'al-Ḥusayn Aḥmad al-Amīnī al-Najafī, vol. 1 (Tehran, 1340 Sh/ 1381 AH/ 1961). (In Persian)

Naqvi, Sayyid Raḍī Ja'far, trans., *Khulāsih-yi al-Ghadīr*, vol. 1 (Lahore, 1410 AH/ 1990). (In Urdu)

Abridged editions of *al-Ghadīr* in Arabic, Persian, and Urdu

Iftikhārzādih, Maḥmūd-Riḍā, Khulāsih-yi al-Ghadīr (Tehran, 1380 Sh/ 2001). (In Persian)

Al-Ḥusaynī al-Kāshānī al-Gharawī, Sayyid Muḥammad 'Alī, abr., *Jur'ah min al-Ghadīr* (Qum, 1431 AH/ 1389 Sh/ 2011). (In Arabic)

Amīnī Najafī, Muḥammad, *Siyrī dar al-Ghadīr* (Qum, 1370 Sh/ 1989) (In Persian); English trans., *An Introduction to al-Ghadīr Books*, trans. Sediqe Bayat (Tehran, 1394 Sh/ 2015).

Amīnī, 'Abd al-Ḥusayn, *Guzīdihyī jāmi' az al-Ghadīr*, abr. by Muḥammad-Ḥasan Shafī'ī Shāhrūdī (Qum, 1386 Sh/ 2007). (In Persian)

Az Ghadīr tā al-Ghadīr: Āshināyī bā Ghadīr wa al-Ghadīr-i Allāma Amīnī (Mashhad, 1389 Sh/ 1431 AH/ 2010). (In Persian)

Dawānī, ʻAlī, *Bih yād-i Allāma Amīnī: Dūrnamā-yī az Kitāb-i guirānqadr-i al-Ghadīr* (Tehran, 1379 Sh/ 2000). (In Persian)

Islāmī, Abū al-Faḍl, *Siyrī dar al-Ghadīr* (Qum, 1379 Sh/ 2000). (In Persian)

Mashkūrī, Muḥammad-Ḥusayn, *Khaṭṭ-i rowshan: Guzīdih-yi Kitāb-i arzishmand-i al-Ghadīr-i Allāma Amīnī* (Qum, 1392 Sh/ 2013). (In Persian)

Miʻrājī, Riḍā, *Hizār nuktih az al-Ghadīr* (Qum, 1391 Sh/ 2012). (In Persian)

Mujābī, Muḥsin, ed., *al-Ghadīr chih mīgūyad* (Qum, 1393 Sh/ 2014). (In Persian)

Qāsimlū, Yaʻqūb, *Khulāṣih-yi al-Ghadīr* (Qum, 1380 Sh/ 2001). (In Persian)

Rizvi Shuʻur Gupalpuri, Syed Ali Akhtar, abr. and trans., *Ghadīr: Qur'an, hadith aur adab min*, 6 vols. (Qum, 1432 AH/ 1389 Sh/ 1010). (In Urdu)

Arabic Indexes to *al-Ghadīr*

Al-Munīr: Fihris kitāb al-Ghadīr (Tehran, 1409 AH/ 1989).

Muḥammadī, ʻAbd Allāh, Muḥammad Bahrihmand, and Muḥammad Muḥaddith, *ʻAlā ḍifāf al-Ghadīr*, ed. by Sayyid Fāḍil al-Mīlānī (Mashhad, 1403 AH/ 1361 Sh/ 1982).

Al-Murawwij al-Khurāsānī, ʻAlī-Aṣghar, *Fi riḥāb al-Ghadīr* (Qum/ Beirut, 1414 AH/ 1993); *Naẓrah ilā al-Ghadīr* (Qum, 1416 AH/ 1995).

Bibliographies of Ghadīr Khumm

Anṣārī-Zanjānī, M., comp., *Ghadīr dar āyīnih-yi kitāb* (Qum, 1390 Sh/ 2011).

Ṭabāṭabā'ī-Yazdī, Sayyid 'Abd al-'Azīz, *al-Ghadīr fī al-turāth al-Islāmī* (Beirut, 1414 AH/ 1993).

www.ingramcontent.com/pod-product-compliance
Lightning Source LLC
Chambersburg PA
CBHW071500080526
44587CB00014B/2165
* 9 7 8 1 9 0 8 1 1 0 5 8 9 *